Praise for Amy \
BIRTH, BREATH, AND .
Motherhood, Chaplaincy, and Life as a Doula

"Amy Wright Glenn has written a remarkable book that I found very touching, reading it as I did when I was caring for my husband during the last weeks of his life. Because she's such a brave soul, I very much enjoyed her company as I journeyed deeper into that territory that had to be traveled."
—*Ina May Gaskin, Midwife and Author of Spiritual Midwifery, Ina May's Guide to Childbirth, and Birth Matters: A Midwife's Manifesta*

"Philosophy, religion and love infuse this thoughtful set of observations."
—*Kirkus Reviews*

"Amy Wright Glenn has brought her own great sensitivity and heart to the portals where we enter and leave this life, and to the loving presence that is our source. Filled with a wisdom that touches into the great mystery, *Birth, Breath, and Death* is a poetic and beautiful reading experience."
—*Tara Brach, PhD, Author of Radical Acceptance and True Refuge*

"Amy Wright Glenn's collection of essays is filled with wisdom that arises from her own life journey as an esteemed high school teacher, inner-city hospital chaplain, birth doula, yoga teacher, daughter, wife, mother, and thoughtful, intuitive human being."
—*Sharon Salzberg, Author of Real Happiness and Lovingkindness*

"The journey that we call 'birth' embraces all the wonders and mystery of life, death, and rebirth. It is a gift that reveals something divine within us, and I think that Amy's book speaks to that gift clearly."
—*Marinah Farrell, President of the Midwives Alliance of North America*

"Becoming a doula, even when she was unsure she wanted to be a mother herself, takes a wide-open mind and heart. Still, I can see why one might become a doula. To help a woman in labor is to be present at a miracle. But to help individuals and their family and friends meet the end is to surround yourself with sadness. That takes a kind of mettle that I cannot fathom but am certainly grateful exists. Amy's willingness to confront death in many forms with fortitude and grace is mind-bending....'We dance between form and formlessness,' she writes. These words made me pause. Yes, so much exists before we are born and after we die. If we're not dancing in between, we are wasting time."
—*Tina Cassidy, Author of Birth: The Surprising History of How We Are Born*

"Rarely is there a book that so deeply touches your soul and has you ponder, celebrate, and revel in life's mysteries and connections. I smiled, prayed, cried, and visioned as I shared Amy Wright Glenn's journey. Her message helped me search deeper into my own life purpose."
—*Debra Pascali-Bonaro, Creator and Director of Orgasmic Birth, Chair of the International MotherBaby Childbirth Organization*

"Reading this book, I am brought ever closer to what I call 'home'—that place of clear seeing and knowing from within,

the place where I deepen my relationship to Self and the world around me."
—*Sudha Carolyn Lundeen, Soulful Life Coach and Senior Kripalu Yoga Teacher Trainer*

"Amy Wright Glenn is a seeker who takes us on an adventurous journey in this compact, insightful, and inspiring book. We travel with her into self-discovery and into the healing of wounds from childhood—the destination is an openhearted motherhood. She has written a lovely book."
—*Kathryn Black, PhD, Author of Mothering Without a Map*

"Lyrical, gentle, contemplative, and touching."
—*Molly Remer, Founder of Talk Birth*

"Amy Wright Glenn has a poet's heart and voice. I recommend *Birth, Breath, and Death* to any person who appreciates well-crafted narratives of growth and transformation, especially those professionals engaged in the work of spiritual and physical nurture."
—*Tedford J. Taylor, Director of Pastoral Care & Training at Robert Wood Johnson University Hospital Hamilton*

"Through stories and personal narrative, Glenn creates an evocative search for meaning, suffusing readers with inspiration and hope for a better self and a better world."
—*International Lactation Consultant Association*®

Birth, Breath, and Death

Meditations on Motherhood, Chaplaincy, and Life as a Doula

Amy Wright Glenn

Text copyright 2013

by AMY WRIGHT GLENN

Copyright © 2014 Amy Wright Glenn
All Rights Reserved

ISBN: 1482079828
ISBN 13: 9781482079821
Library of Congress Control Number: 2013902206
CreateSpace Independent Publishing Platform
North Charleston, South Carolina

Names and identifying descriptions of those mentioned in the doula and chaplaincy stories have been changed.

For Clark with love abiding
and for Taber with gratitude unending.

*

I honor all who have crossed my path and
lifted me up with kindness.

...you are most certainly an infinitesimal in the cold vastness of the cosmos, and yes, you are only one of billions of humans and other creatures who have come before and will come after, and your life is barely a mathematical instant in the span of time. But you are also--just as certainly--a miracle: you are a creature capable of thought, of wonder, of awe. You are a creature capable of recognizing that you are not the center of the Universe. And it is because of that very capacity that you can see in other people the same intrinsic value that you see in yourself. You are a miracle. You are capable of love, and so need not despair of insignificance.

—Yorke Brown, Dartmouth Professor of Physics and Astronomy

Table of Contents

Introduction

My first year in college, I dreamt my father gave me the keys to The Celestial Kingdom. The energy around us felt calm and holy. I received his gift with awe, respect, and gratitude. A golden ring held together the large, beautiful, and ornate keys to paradise. My father's heavenly offering rested in my hands. For some time, I examined their intricate beauty. In the dream, I gave them back to him. "Dad," I said, "I plan to forge my own."

Years later, while visiting family in Utah, my father wrote me a heartfelt letter as a Christmas gift. It contained his testimony of Jesus Christ. How could I accept it? I remembered my dream and received his gift with kindness. I didn't return the letter to him as I had with the mystical keys. Instead, I silently acknowledged our different conceptions of life's wonders. I am forging my own way. My own understanding of sacred mysteries continues to evolve and deepen. My heart makes room for all lovingly crafted keys and letters.

What makes some embrace inherited traditions while others sojourn into foreign lands? Why search outside of what is given?

I searched.

On my journey, I fell in love with mystical literature, meditation, and the musings of saints. Through my studies, I made illuminating connections between my academic background in comparative religion and philosophy to the work of motherhood, chaplaincy, and being a doula.

While retaining various insights from my faith of origin, I continue to construct my own response to life's profound beauty, pain, and mystery. I am transfixed by love's intensity and power. I am captivated by the study of life's thresholds. What is more mysterious than the great unknown existing beyond the frontiers of birth and death? Through the bodies of women, we are all born into time and space. Each one of us must also walk through that great, uncharted door of death.

A daily practice of meditation and yoga affirms the powerful potential held in each breath. Linking birth with death, breath joins the bookends of human life. After two decades of body/mind-centered healing practice, I know that conscious breathing can open the heart. Love illuminates the mystery of these thresholds.

As a birth doula and a hospital chaplain, I am a confidant to women and men in the throes of liminal and transformative openings. It is an honor beyond measure to offer strength to birthing women as they open to welcome newly created life. Holding the hands of the dying and offering compassion to grieving loved ones is humbling and transformative work. The stories of my hospital chaplaincy training and doula work remain poignant and powerful teachers.

Tonight, I hold my sleeping son in my arms. I want to completely open my heart so I don't miss the wonder of these precious years. Choosing to become a mother involved overcoming great obstacles. I had to directly face the fear inherited from my past. Giving birth to my son profoundly transformed me. Over the first year of his life, I deeply reflected upon the connections between birth, breath, and death. After breathing my way through fear, I found myself in a place of profound and visceral love, the most precious of life's gifts. Motherhood is its own threshold.

You hold in your hands the best of my reflections thus far. I write from the heart of a seeker of truth. I write from the heart of a mother, a most tender place. May the following insights offer you inspiration as you ponder the significance of each human birth, our inevitable encounter with death, and each precious breath. Take what works for you. Draw freely from my perceptions. May my stories give impetus to your crafting of sacred keys.

Search

I am the eldest of seven children raised in a small town in Utah. We lived on an acre of land on a quiet dead-end street. Horse chestnut, linden, and apple trees surrounded our modest home, providing shade and beauty. Farming, rodeo, country music, and pickup trucks were prominent fixtures in my Intermountain Region youth. The majestic Mount Timpanogos served as nature's grand sentinel over our valley. From our front porch, we watched her snowcapped status shift through the seasons. I grew up loving the land and clean mountain air.

Every summer, my father planted rows of tomatoes, corn, potatoes, carrots, and the predictable overabundance of zucchini in our backyard garden. My siblings and I helped in this endeavor. We weeded the large garden and picked out the rocks from the rugged soil. I marveled at nature's wonder as the corn stretched up to the sky. My mother canned and froze much of this food so it would last throughout the year. We knew all of our neighbors and shared any plethora of produce freely.

The Church of Jesus Christ of Latter-day Saints (LDS), also known as the Mormon Church, provided my family with a comforting cocoon of mythology, ritual, and tradition. We marked the major milestones of life with Mormon rituals: baptism at age eight, a Temple marriage when couples pledge fidelity for this life and beyond, and a mission to spread the Gospel. Abundant or at least adequate procreation was expected.

Everyone agreed on how my life should proceed. All of the adults in my family were committed to helping me win salvation. I felt like a character in a story with predetermined plotlines. For my parents, the mantle of upstanding Mormon womanhood didn't depend on attaining a college degree or a certain financial status. I simply needed to nurture my inherited testimony and remain steadfastly loyal to the faith of my pioneering past.

We were a working-class family of nine living in a three-bedroom, one-bath abode. Our house was loud, crowded, and full of life's vicissitudes. Mornings in the bathroom, as we prepped for school, bordered on chaotic. We didn't have very much money, so items of use passed down the line. At times, my parents needed outside support. Not everyone wore used clothes and drove old cars, but we did. Not everyone stood in line to get the free government cheese available at a local elementary school, but sometimes my mom did that too.

In later years, upon learning of my Utah roots, friends asked me where I liked to ski. The truth is I never learned the basic snowplow until my senior year of high school. Skiing expenses far exceeded my father's working-class income. Despite our financial struggles, each additional member of our family was welcomed warmly. Church members brought over homemade meals and visiting relatives added to the festivities. My mother always said her greatest joy in life came with each birth.

In nearly all of my childhood memories, my mother is pregnant or nursing. I have only one vivid childhood memory of my mother apart from pregnancy. She is pushing me on a swing on a warm summer day at our home in American Fork,

Utah. She moves happily in her slender body. The wind tousles her freely flowing hair. She looks beautiful. As we play, she laughs.

I treasure the happy memories I have of my mother, an intense and troubled Mormon woman. At her best, she taught me to bravely stand up for the underdog and to challenge prejudice. "I don't care if a person is polka-dotted; you treat them with respect," she often said. She was a stay-at-home mom and breastfed all of us as infants. She devoted hours a day to cooking wholesome and comforting meals for our large family.

At the age of eleven, I watched an interview with Geraldine Ferraro, a candidate for the US vice presidency. "I might be a Democrat," I told my mother as she stood by the sink washing dishes. To her everlasting credit, she calmly listened as I did my best to summarize Ferraro's key points. We lived in Utah, a sea of Republican red, but she encouraged me to think such things through for myself. I cherish the positive gifts she provided.

However, great fear and sadness moved through the woman who brought me into this life. Although she solemnly affirmed, "Patriarchy is the will of God," submitting to such paternal power brought her little peace. My mother struggled deeply with an inner confusion and darkness that color my memories of her with sadness. While I may have been free to question commonly held political assumptions, challenging Mormon doctrine was unthinkable. "If you leave the Church, Amy, it would be better if you had never been born." For many years, these words haunted me. Her worldview consisted of a pitched battle between the forces of good and the forces of evil. Somehow our home became ground zero. At one point, she was convinced that ants found in a bedroom closet heralded the efforts of Satan who supposedly longed to possess members of my family.

Tragically, moments of simple happiness, even in the presence of her children, became increasingly rare. My mother's privately guarded depression and growing delusional paranoia permeated the daily rhythms of our household. Increasingly drawn to a literal interpretation of the scarier sides of LDS theology, she too often focused on fear rather than love. I don't blame Mormonism for the way she focused on otherworldly, nightmarish signs regarding the Last Days. Due to her bio-chemistry, I believe she would have homed in on the darker sides of any religious tradition.

One evening, we stood outside next to the walnut tree in our backyard. A grey full moon orbited calmly in the darkening sky. "Amy, come here," my mother said. I walked closer. "Do you see that moon?" she asked. I nodded, following the direction of her pointing hand. I shifted uncomfortably in my shoes, taking note of the ominous energy in her voice. "One day the moon will turn to blood. When you see this happen, no matter where you are, you must come home immediately. It will turn blood red. Do you hear me?" Her body stiffened with the gravity of this gruesome teaching. She looked into my eyes with a piercing focus. My stomach turned into a knot.

"Sure Mom. OK." I nodded, looking away from her. I longed for the conversation to quickly end.

Even then, I knew something was wrong with her. Religious paranoia provides no nourishment for a child. Literal renderings of Manichean-style teachings only obstruct clear seeing. I didn't need to check the sky for lunar signs of apocalyptic fright. The moon wouldn't turn to blood. Why didn't she teach me about gravitational pull or eclipses? Why not simply savor the grandeur of a giant, harmless, rock floating in space? Why so much fear?

As I grew, I strengthened my resolve to protect my younger siblings from her religiously colored paranoia. Attempting to mend this mother wound, I counterbalanced the grim energy with cheerful play. "Call me Big Amy!" I declared as I filled our days with creative adventure.

We secretly explored the precariously arranged haystacks in our neighbor's barn. We conquered dragons, built elaborate blanket forts, and imagined surviving Armageddon with seventy-two-hour survival kits in tow. Our mother's focus on eschatology and the Mormon Church's dictum to store a year's supply of food in our basement mixed together. Apocalyptic games made perfect sense.

Neighborhood pranks involved copious amounts of toilet paper. Sleeping out in the backyard under the stars was a highlight of summer nights. Most of our play took place in our acre lot of trees nestled both behind our house and next to the roaring I-15 freeway. This familiar thoroughfare served as an aorta for motor vehicles linking Utah together on its north/south axis.

By the time I was fourteen, I began to challenge Mormon theology. At one point, I went to my ward bishop with burning questions. He listened with kindness and promised to discuss my relentless doubts at an undetermined future date. Though wise from years of farming and raising large families, my Mormon elders didn't know quite what to do with me. Perhaps they imagined my skepticism and spiritual quandaries were due to adolescent angst. The bishop never got back to me. Regretfully, I never summoned the courage to remind him of his promise.

After hearing one of the Mormon apostles declare that "intellectuals, feminists, and homosexuals" constituted the three greatest threats to the Church, I knew the carefully crafted LDS worldview could no longer hold back my seeking mind and heart. I didn't fear homosexuality, and I bravely considered myself a budding intellectual feminist thanks to my high school AP Biology teacher, who mentored me. I began to imagine the world on the other side of the Wasatch Front mountain range.

So I decided to stop attending church. This choice was met with immediate consequences. Many of the weekly privileges I enjoyed while living in my parents' house depended on Sunday church activity. For example, if I wanted to use the phone during the week, I had to attend church and earn that privilege. My parents couldn't force me to go to church, but they could restrict my free time. Missing church meant I was grounded at home after school. Weekends were suddenly family-only time. At first, I tried not to care about the restrictions. On Sunday mornings, I reveled in the quiet of being home alone. I could listen to music, dance, and read without a single distraction. This rarely happened given the eight other inhabitants who shared close quarters with me. However the novelty soon wore off and I missed spending time with my friends. "Dad, we need to talk," I said one Saturday evening. I hoped he would be open to a compromise.

After a difficult and honest conversation, my father and I made a pact. Although my father believed that the LDS church embodied the full truth, he also thought that aspects of truth could be found in all faiths. Therefore, he agreed that I could attend any of the small non-Mormon churches in our community and it would "count" as if I had been to the LDS church. I gratefully accepted this open-minded solution to our impasse. My father cautiously encouraged my budding spiritual exploration. He remained confident that I would return to the faith of my ancestors.

From Baptist revivals and Pentecostal healings to Catholic Mass, I dove headfirst into Utah's fascinating religious landscape outside of Mormonism. While I found much beauty in Christian mythology, I steered clear of Biblical literalism. Instead, I was drawn to Eastern traditions. In particular, I fell in love with meditation and chanting. I was surprised to discover an elaborate Hare Krishna temple an hour's drive from my home complete with its own herd of llamas. It soon became my favored Sunday destination spot. At that temple, I learned to link dance with prayer.

As a child, I loved dancing with my younger siblings. Most forms of rock music were contraband in my family's house, so we danced to country music and reenacted scenes from musicals, our favorite being Stanley Donen's 1954 hit *Seven Brides for Seven Brothers*. Rodgers and Hammerstein scores and LDS hymns poured out of the speakers in our small living room. My mother said I loved dancing even as a toddler. She said she used to dance with me then. I wish I could remember those years because I have no memory of my mother dancing. Today when I dance, I envision her joining me, finally moving freely. I like to imagine all of my Mormon ancestors cutting loose. I conjure up my mother dancing, for her breath is in my bones. I transform it through dance.

As a teen, I loved dancing through various stages of rebellion. However, I soon discovered that clubs, mirrors, alcohol, revealing clothing, and techno beats could obscure the spiritual power inherent in dance. The seamless combination of movement and divine supplication came alive for me during Hare Krishna *pujas*, or worship services. Watching bodies express the heart's deepest longing for communion changed me. One could dance and pray at the same time? Prayer merged with music. I danced sadness, strength, friendship, peace, and joy. As the Muslim mystic Rumi wrote, "He who knoweth the dance, dwelleth in God."

Earth-based religions had much to teach me. I traveled with a few daring high school friends to Nevada where we joined an international protest against nuclear weapon testing on Native American land. The weekend consisted of long philosophical talks around campfires and lots of drumming. Native-American-inspired morning rituals welcomed the sun. While in Nevada, I received my first therapeutic massage. As the therapist worked through areas of various muscle tension in my shoulders, I started crying. Clearly my body held unnecessary tension, fear, and stress. I vowed to further explore this healing modality and work toward integration. I returned to Utah on fire with newfound insights.

I wasn't alone in my search. I found spiritual kinship in the company of progressive dreamers, visionaries, activists, artists, and renegades.

✺

My journey led me to formally study comparative religion and philosophy in college. I was the first person in my immediate family to complete a four-year degree. I received generous educational grants, making my studies possible. My parents were proud of my success and my father took special interest in my studies of religion.

While a student at Reed College in Oregon, I maintained a beginner's-level meditation practice, which consisted of relaxing visualizations and simple techniques that calmed my inner world. I also started a yoga *asana* practice, the mindful physical movements for which yoga is most well known. My yoga teacher was a dynamic, petite, Catholic mother of five. She taught me how to do a headstand and bolstered my confidence as I conquered my fear of falling. At a college like Reed, known for its intensity and intellectual rigor, these practices brought needed balance. Over time, they powerfully transformed me.

One day at Reed, I walked out of a dry lecture on various literary themes present in the Bible. I found a quiet place to be alone in the campus woods and imagined what my maternal grandmother would have thought of the professor's secular Biblical criticism. I cried my heart out. The juxtaposition hurt.

At the time, I was the only student at Reed who had been raised a Mormon. Reed's tongue-in-cheek unofficial motto -- "Communism, Atheism, and Free Love" -- didn't resonate with me. The discord between my family's faith and the nearly universal campus-wide atheism made me feel lonely. My college professors served as wise academic mentors, but I needed spiritual support. Studying philosophy and religion is not the same as practicing it. I longed to experience community rituals and missed the presence of elders and new babies in my life.

Even though I respected Mormonism's unique approach to the ineffable, I was critical of the corruption found in the repression of feminine intuition and curious minds. LDS theology no longer resonated with me, but I really missed going to church. I longed for a viable means of marking significant milestones in life. I missed having a way to honor the rites of passage and rituals of life: weddings, funerals, births, and deaths. I yearned for a spiritually conscious community that welcomed my intellectual curiosity, honored the wisdom found in all world religions, and danced together to healing rhythms.

I found Portland's Unitarian Universalist First Church through my interest in poetry. Marilyn Sewell, the editor of my favorite poetry anthology, which focused on women's spirituality, lived in Portland. I heard she was the minister at First Church and woke early one Sunday to attend. Alone, I navigated my way downtown on Portland's public transit bus system. Reverend Sewell led a coming-of-age ceremony for three teenaged members of the congregation. The simplicity of the ritual, the absence of patriarchal dogma that would prohibit a woman from offering such a blessing, and her grounded presence touched me deeply.

I was drawn to the way that Unitarian Universalist (UU) ministers attempt to evoke wonder and exploration in the minds and hearts of their congregants. William Ellery Channing, a famous 19th century Unitarian minister wrote, "The great end in religious instruction is not to impose religion." Channing urged religious leaders not to "stamp our minds upon the young but to stir up their own." From that point forward, the UU community became an integral part of my spiritual nourishment. By affirming and promoting ethical standards that advocate a "free and responsible search for truth and meaning," First Church offered a community that embraced an open-hearted and intellectually inquisitive approach to life.

To complement my studies, I spent much of my early twenties traveling throughout the Middle East and India. I lost track of time gazing at an ancient copy of Homer's *Iliad* at a museum in Cairo. I remember sleeping through a freezing cold night on Mt. Sinai and awakening to a brilliant sunrise over the Arabian Peninsula. I climbed the pyramids in Egypt and protested the Israeli occupation of the West Bank with Arab and Jewish women peace activists. For a year, I studied in Jerusalem. Later, I dedicated myself to the practice of meditation at an ashram in the Himalayas.

A lively mix of debate and discussion characterized my Hebrew University days. In the evenings, I worked illegally as a waitress in the Jewish Quarter of the Old City. Adorned in Roman attire, I served fantastic platters of Middle Eastern cuisine and performed folk songs and dance routines for photo-snapping tourists. I was nineteen and living in Jerusalem, a place saturated in religious symbolism. Known as *Al-Quds* in Arabic and *Yerushalim* in Hebrew, Jerusalem is a city renewed and ravaged due to contested paradigms of poetry and politics.

I loved the quiet walk back to my dorm room on Mount Scopus. It provided needed personal space for reflection. The cool evening air provided relief after a hectic night of waitressing, dancing, and smiling for the camera. Jerusalem's famous panoply of holy sites inspired reflections about the nature of reality, God, and mystery. In particular, the *Haram al Sharif*, or Temple Mount, mesmerized me. All religions offer different doorways into the mystical silence encountered in meditation. All religious dogmas can be used to exclude and justify inflicting harm. There's nothing like living in Jerusalem to come to know both of these statements as truth.

One late afternoon, I noticed an unusually radiant group of people completing a bar mitzvah celebration at the Kotel, or Western Wall. Because this festive Jewish rite of passage occurs multiple times a day at the Kotel, I simply registered their presence. However, a deeper instinct drew me toward them. Trusting these intuitions, I introduced myself. They were Canadian but currently lived in India, where they studied at a meditation center in the Himalayas. They were only in Jerusalem for a few days to celebrate the bar mitzvah and would soon return to India. That night they planned to gather for a group meditation. They asked if I'd like to join them. "Of course! Thank you so much," I replied.

Later that evening, I sat on a blanket in a beautifully landscaped courtyard with thirty or so kindred souls. The woman who led the meditation directed our attention to the presence of a silent, safe, infinite space within us. She told us to bring awareness to the physical body first. Then she guided us to rest our attention on the breath. Finally, a calming mantra enabled me to let go of all thought, all sound, and eventually the mantra itself. What was left? The silence between sensations, breaths, and thoughts. This silent, peaceful space connected each one of us to all of life and to its remarkable wonders.

Throughout my studies, I loved reflecting upon people's vivid descriptions of mystical visions of unity. Ralph Waldo Emerson wrote, "Within us is the soul of the Whole, the wise silence, the universal beauty, to which every part and particle is equally related; the Eternal One." However, it is one thing to study an idea and quite another to experience it. To paraphrase philosopher Ken Wilber, you wouldn't eat a menu and call it lunch, right? Zen Buddhist wisdom reminds adherents not to confuse the finger pointing to the moon with the moon itself. One could spend years studying the mechanics of swimming, but until one slips into the wetness of water, only an intellectual sliver of what it means to swim is ascertained. Gathered around me were individuals fully committed to experiencing the vision Emerson described and diving headfirst into the Eternal One.

We sat for an hour in silence. I was enveloped by a peace such that I had never known. Meditation came alive and the healing energy of an all-pervading love surrounded me. As a child, when touching the edges of this deep love, I attributed it to the power of Jesus Christ. On that transformative evening at a friendly stranger's home, an essential metaphysical insight unfolded. I had been raised to acknowledge only one entrance to God's energy. In fact, one need not use the term "God" at all. Such a term is another doorway into the mysterious heart unifying all existence. However, humans need language to direct the attention to the ineffable. There are many names for this mystery. The doorways were holy, too. In this sense, the calming, silent, spacious energy discovered in my meditation both transcended Christ and was Christ.

I began to cry, and the pain of my separation from Mormonism ran down my cheeks as tears. I sat in a timeless quiescence of connection. My past and my present united. My religious upbringing focused on devotional prayer. There I sat, focusing on the space behind, between, and permeating throughout all prayer. Prayers formed by the child's heart within me and this new space merged as one. Connected to the surrounding meditators, the tree roots below, the stars circling millions of miles above, and my family in Utah, I fell into Christ and the abiding holy and vast silence. They were one. People travel for miles to seek the counsel of holy ones. Now I only needed to devote myself to a daily practice of going within, a daily practice of breathing Jesus.

Later that year, I traveled alone to India to study meditation. Traversing India's vibrant, wild, difficult, and colorful landscape was an overwhelming experience. I met up with my Jerusalem friends in the northern Indian state of Himachal Pradesh. The swami in charge of their ashram purposely built the meditation center right next to a congested main road to strengthen the community's practice of diving into silence in the midst of our cacophonous world, and it worked.

Over the next few years, I took my practice of seated meditation very seriously. I spent hours a day in silence and returned to this ashram two more times for deeper study. I benefited greatly from the swami's teachings of Advaita Vedanta, a Hindu philosophy that affirmed the oneness I had experienced in Jerusalem. I conducted scholarly research through lengthy interviews with ashram residents and focused my senior thesis at Reed on Advaita Vedanta. Whether meditating in India or Portland, the space within remained a constant, softening, and welcoming peace. All I needed was a safe place to sit and close my eyes. Upon opening them, I saw the daily forms of human life more clearly as miracles.

*

Throughout human history, seekers of love and truth have embarked on long pilgrimages. Even today, hundreds of millions travel to holy sites to perform rituals, visit the graves of poets and saints, and sit at the feet of living masters. Muslims circle the Ka'ba, Hindus bathe in the river Ganges, Catholics walk the Camino de Santiago, Jews pray at the Kotel, and Mormons conduct temple work.

I love this diverse tapestry of religious expression, yet I join mystics everywhere in affirming a central truth. The holiest journey leads the pilgrim into the depths of the human heart. One must simply dive inside. There it is. Love imbues all experience, including silence and sound, form and emptiness. Hurt, pain, and anger are acknowledged, honored, and more deeply understood due to spiritual practice.

According to philosopher Ken Wilber, we find "deep structures" at every level of human experience. Deep structures are transcultural facts of our existence. We also discover "surface structures" contingent upon culture, time, and context. For example, one deep structure is the form of the human body itself. Except in cases of rare genetic mutations, human bodies have one heart, two kidneys, two lungs, one nose, etc. Surface structures include the various ways people care for and adorn their bodies. The abilities to think, create language, and form meaningful symbols constitute the deep structures on the level of the mind. Our world's linguistic and philosophical diversity attests to the range of the mind's surface structures.

Wilber posits that deep and surface structures also apply to the realm of the spirit. Underlying the diversity of forms found in this universe is one vibrant power and energy. On the surface level, there are variations in religious dogma, spiritual practice, revelation, and sacred scriptures. The deep structure of the spirit is realized when the illusion between subject and object dissolves. Experiencing the wonder of this unifying power opens the door to what mythologist Joseph Campbell calls the "ultimate truth." Campbell posits that myth and ritual can only be the "penultimate truth." Nothing in human language or in art can adequately express the immensity of the one energy that underlies existence.

Spiritual surface structures open human beings to encounters with the ineffable. For example, given my Mormon background, calling the spacious mystery of meditation "Christ," as I did in Jerusalem, helped open my heart to its fullness. But the mystery transcends all words. My father and I don't have to rely on the same keys to a heavenly kingdom in order to love and respect one another. I have no doubt that when my father bows his head in a small Utah town and when I meditate in quiet sublime stillness, we touch the same source. At their best, religious traditions affirm the wonder at the heart of existence and provide meaningful contexts for its experience. This mystery allows us to breathe, dream, love, and dimly perceive something beyond time even while we live in time.

My days of conquering dragons in the acre lot of trees behind my childhood home now exist only in memories and dreams. Meditation, inspiring scholarship, and finding a spiritual home brought needed healing and insight. I searched and forged my own keys to a grand inner kingdom. Today, I make space in my heart to transform lingering fears. The moon is simply the moon, a miracle enough.

Labor Sleepover

When she was six months pregnant, my younger sister, Rachel, faced a painful marital separation. It proved too much for her to bear alone. She needed calm, security, friendship, and loving support. So did her soon-to-be-born daughter. My husband, Clark, and I opened our home and welcomed her with joy. She lived with us during the final trimester of her pregnancy, the birth, and the postpartum recovery.

Before she arrived, she called me. "Amy, will you be my birth partner?" she asked. I said yes. It was an answer that would change my life.

I projected confidence, yet inside I felt nervous, hesitant, and out of place. Although I could outline the basic philosophies of various world religions, I knew next to nothing about childbirth. How could I support her through this rite of passage into motherhood?

While checking out a few books on birthing, I shared these fears with the librarian. "Have you considered hiring a doula?" she inquired. I had never heard this word before. Gratefully, she took a break from her work to educate me about the services that doulas provide birthing women.

The word "doula" comes from a Greek term meaning "woman servant." Today, doulas master the art of providing skilled comfort measures to ease the pain of birth. They lovingly aid and attend to women in labor. Doulas stand at the doorway of life. They support birthing women as they transform into open vessels. Although the aim of midwives or an obstetric medical team is to safeguard the health of the mother and the child, a doula focuses on the mother. A doula mothers the mother.

I wanted to hire a doula for Rachel. Later that afternoon, I met up with her and enthusiastically shared my new discovery.

She laughed and said, "Amy, I don't need a doula. I have you!"

I paused. "Well, I need a doula."

So, she humored me. We hired a doula. Rachel's midwife fully supported us in bringing a doula on board. We found a wonderful woman, full of passion for her work. As a former opera singer, she sang like an angel. Her calming and beautiful melodies brought a great deal of peace to the early hours of labor.

When Rachel knocked on our bedroom door at 5:30 am on a late March morning, I bolted upright. My beloved niece was soon to be born. Knowing our doula would arrive at our request brought tremendous relief and calmed any lingering trepidation. I wouldn't be alone in supporting Rachel through the trials ahead. Our doula joined us for the vast majority of Rachel's twenty-four-hour labor. Her helpful, kind, and informed presence proved invaluable.

Rachel quickly morphed into the bravest person I knew. Wonder and pain mixed into a strong elixir coursing through my sister's beautiful body. We spent hours walking through the springtime fields behind our home. She labored in the upstairs tub as water washed over her rhythmic contractions. At the hospital, she moaned and rocked and said she felt agonizing pressure. She cried and bled. I massaged her body as she mercifully rested during the five-minute respites between contractions. These respites are nature's wise gift to birthing women.

At one point as Rachel rested between pushing, our midwife turned to me and said, "You'd be a good doula." Her words fell into the fertile soil of soon-to-be-manifested dreams.

Then Rachel's cervix opened fully and the downward pressure compelled action. While pushing, she compressed every bone in my hand. I didn't dare say anything given what was happening to her vagina. The baby crowned. Then, with a hearty push, new life slipped out of Rachel's watery, warm womb. A threshold opened, and my sister gave birth.

The energy in the room shifted with celebratory grace and tearful smiles. We welcomed this precious one to the earthly realm of gravity, air, and land. Rachel's body handled the birth beautifully. She remained conscious, informed, and connected to the process even in the most difficult moments. Birth brings powerful and painful sensations to the most intimate spaces of the female body. My sister opened to this reality. I stood transfixed by the life-giving strength found in her feminine power. I certainly held a newfound respect for the vagina.

"A woman's body knows what to do," our midwife stated in the most matter-of-fact way.

All female mammals give birth. However, only human women experience an extraordinary intensifying of labor pains because of our species' unique hip-to-head ratio, the product of bipedalism and brainpower. Given this, women rarely give birth alone. For generations, women risked their lives to bring the next generation into this world. Even today in many parts of the world, complications in childbirth too often prove fatal.

After being Rachel's birth partner, I understood the invaluable gifts a doula can bring to a birthing mother. Trained to listen and love, such women hold, caress, and encourage a mother to courageously open to her primal nature. Hour-by-hour support nourishes a woman's trust in her body's organic timetable for giving birth. Honoring the unique flow of each woman's time in labor is vital if the mother hopes to birth her child in the most natural way possible. To birth as nature intended triggers a cascade of hormones that assist mother-child attachment. A doula's encouragement helps a woman trust her own power. Body and breath awareness aid a woman in her capacity to accept and engage with the power of birth.

Following Rachel's birth experience, I devoted myself to doula training, which led to my acceptance as a Doulas of North America (DONA)-certified birth doula. The DONA vision is to ensure "a doula for every woman who wants one." This vision inspires a concrete set of mission statements directed at training a cadre of skilled doulas working to improve the well-being of mother and child in childbirth and the postpartum period.

A doula can provide numerous benefits. A couple may hire a doula because they are uncertain about the process. They may know their limits well enough to ask for extra support. Hiring a doula is an extraordinary way for the parents to care for each other. The birth partner is also supported in his or her role of caring for the mother during childbirth. If the labor is particularly trying, long, difficult, or emotionally charged, the doula and the birth partner can take breaks and help each other support the mother. Multiple medical studies show that the number of requests for pain-relieving medicines decreases when a couple receives comforting measures and emotional encouragement from a doula. Pain doesn't have to equal suffering. Embodying this wisdom is the work of a doula.

At the time of Rachel's delivery, I worked in the Religion and Philosophy Department at The Lawrenceville School in New Jersey. Known for its beautiful campus, excellent teaching, and talented students, Lawrenceville is one of the best boarding schools in the US. The high school students I taught during my eleven years there astounded me with their creativity, beauty, and intelligence. I truly loved my job. Given that so much of my own inner questioning blossomed in my high school years, I felt called to offer loving, accepting, and inspiring energy to teens. This didn't change when I became a doula even though I took breaks from grading my ever-expanding pile of student papers in order to read about best practices in providing labor support.

Becoming a doula added to my work reflecting on life's essential questions with my Lawrenceville students. At times, I even taught classes energized by the high of witnessing the miracle of an all-night birthing experience. Supporting the emergence of a child from the round, full bodies of birthing women helped me see my own students with a clarion vision. Once, they had been held in the arms of an exhausted but triumphant mother. This fact renewed my efforts to provide them with the best possible teaching I could summon.

Linking my work as a doula to lectures on Middle East history didn't work. But my beloved Myth and Ritual class provided ample opportunity to connect various theories about rites of passage to the remarkable stories of birth. In particular, I loved introducing my students to the scholarship of Joseph Campbell. Together we applied his three-tiered description of the classic hero's journey to the process of birth. In Campbell's description, a hero departs from the known world; experiences various trials, revelations, and fulfillment; and finally returns to the community bringing spiritual or physical gifts for renewal. Not only does this apply to the hero motif present in world mythology, but it also relates to the experiences of every birthing woman. When labor begins, a woman departs from the known world. She crosses over the threshold of normal life into what many birthing professionals call "Labor Land". The trials faced and revelations obtained through the process of birth transform a woman and offer her fulfillment. She returns to her community with the twin gifts of her own deepened vision and the wonder of a new life.

My students benefited from these real-life connections. Not many high school teachers are certified doulas. I enjoyed making links between the hours spent at the hospital and the hours spent in the classroom. Our studies of creation myths and naming rituals took on a fuller significance when we imagined all of us as once helpless, trusting, naked little creatures, beauty incarnate. We also reflected upon our shared journey through the mysteries of life ending with the encounter with death.

Aztec elders taught that women who died in childbirth went to the same level of paradise as men who died in battle. After attending over forty births, I fully understood why. Men die in battle from intense wounds. They bleed as they sacrifice for a greater cause. The same holds true for women who die in childbirth. They bleed as they open to life. The juxtaposition of beauty and pain in each birth astounds me. Each story lives in me.

✧

Divya asked me to be the doula for the birth of her second child. She and her husband, Samuel, lived in the concrete-block housing units provided to Princeton University's graduate students. In preparation for the birth, I met with them twice. Surrounded by bookshelves teeming with Samuel's dissertation research, we discussed their hopes and fears regarding the upcoming birth. A few weeks later, we cleared away the front room furniture so I could teach a prenatal yoga class to the couple.

Years of practicing yoga combined with my love of teaching and I became a certified yoga teacher in 2002. After becoming a doula, I sought out special certification for prenatal yoga teaching. I know how much wisdom, love, and pain are stored in the body. Teaching yoga to doula clients in preparation for birth greatly aids my understanding of how they work as a couple, how the mother moves in her body, and how I can best offer hands-on support during labor.

Doula work is very much like teaching yoga. In yoga, the teacher brings attention to breath, to tired muscles, to emotional blockages, and to the free space between moments of tension. With gentleness, I guide my yoga students to experience the wisdom within their own bodies. Doula work is similar to teaching yoga except doula work is equivalent to a twenty-to-thirty-hour-long class.

On a full moon night in mid-January, Divya's labor began. I was on my way to teach a yoga class when Samuel called. For the past few hours, Divya's contractions had been ten or so minutes apart. The intensity had increased but the rhythm had remained the same. Knowing that this could go on for many more hours, I decided to continue on to my class, but I put my phone on vibrate just in case. The upcoming birth inspired me to guide thirty yoga practitioners through a series of asanas that honored birth. Together, we held *jai asana,* also known as the victory squat or goddess pose, in honor of the mother to be. After all, Divya was practicing the most holy form of yoga, one as ancient as days.

At 11 pm, Divya called. The ten-minute contraction pattern continued like a steady labor dance. She hesitated to ask me to come over in case this wasn't "the real deal."

It was early labor, but I wanted to be there to support her. I suggested she take a shower, relax, and allow the unfolding to begin. "I'll be there within the hour," I told her.

I arrived at her home before midnight. Divya and Samuel were downstairs. They greeted me with warm hugs and cheerful words. At first glance, one never would have known Divya was in labor. Yet every ten minutes, she intuitively found her way to her knees. She needed the steady, grounding earth to help her open to the increasingly strong sensations moving through her body. Kneeling, she rocked and moaned through the waves of contractions that were building and releasing.

Most likely, the labor would continue all night. I suggested that Samuel get some sleep. I would work with Divya so she could sleep, or at least rest well, between contractions. They both needed their energy. It was best to conserve it now. Samuel packed the car before heading to bed. Divya enjoyed a glass of red wine "to take the edge off," she said. While such a practice may seem unorthodox, many midwives I know commonly recommend a glass of wine in early labor. Divya smiled as she raised her glass to toast the occasion. Her magical, full-moon birthing had begun.

For the next seven hours, Divya and I had what we later called "a labor sleepover." We rested next to each other on the guest bed and fell into whatever sleep our bodies could sustain for ten-minute intervals. When her contractions began, I helped Divya move through the intensity of the building sensations with calming words. Unable to recline during her increasingly powerful contractions, Divya awoke, rolled onto her knees, swayed, moaned, and breathed. I applied pressure during contractions to the muscles around her sacrum; this low back massage offered her marked relief. I also used a simple technique from Central America involving a labor shawl called a *rebozo*. When Divya moved to her hands and knees, I wrapped the rebozo around her lower abdomen, below her pregnant belly. I held onto both ends of the cloth, skillfully lifting and rocking with her as she worked through the contractions. The extra support minimizes muscle pain around the pelvis.

A full moon moved incrementally across the horizon. Gentle lunar light steadily washed over the white snow while Divya labored to bring forth her beloved child. As her doula, I held sacred space for her. I mothered the mother and watched the moon move across the winter sky. Our labor sleepover dance between rest and birth work continued all night.

The sun started to rise in the form of soft pink light. Morning came and Divya's contraction pattern continued. Samuel awoke recharged for the upcoming day. He took over as birth partner, and I went home to sleep until the labor pattern intensified and they needed my help again. Around 10 am, Samuel and Divya drove to their midwife's office for a previously scheduled appointment. Around 11 am, Samuel called. The baby's heartbeat was healthy and strong, and Divya's cervix was dilated five centimeters and 100 percent effaced. This news was wonderful. Before pushing can begin, a cervix must dilate to ten centimeters. It also thins, or effaces, to provide a passageway for the baby. Taking the advice of their midwife, Divya and Samuel decided to head directly to the hospital.

I got up from my much-needed morning rest and showered. I met the couple around noon. The labor and delivery room was painted predictable shades of soft pastels. It was full of beeping machines that remained quiet through Divya's birth experience. Divya wanted a natural birth. Together with her midwife, Samuel, and me, the hospital nurses offered loving support. Natural birth is rare in contemporary American hospitals; therefore, a certain excitement filled the air. Divya's cervix was now dilated seven centimeters. The baby continued the descent into the pelvis.

"All will be well," Samuel said, invoking the wisdom of Saint Julian of Norwich, who famously wrote, "All will be well. All will be well. All manner of things will be well."

Patience, time, and kindness assisted the process unfolding in rhythmic waves in Divya's body. Walking also helped tremendously. A 4:30 pm trip to the Jacuzzi offered ancient and soothing relief. Water is a "liquid midwife" according to novelist Bem Le Hunte, and its warm healing properties surrounded Divya's fully fertile form.

Divya made strong sounds and felt powerful emotions accompany the rhythmic physical pain. Samuel prayed, and we both offered hands-on support. Divya had torn terribly during her first birth experience and needed surgery to repair her vagina. She feared she would repeat this trauma. Understandably, she wanted to avoid tearing again. The midwife was concerned about the elasticity of the scar tissue. I breathed with Divya and together we made a space for the fear. We focused on fortitude and the need to carry on. "Courage, dear Divya," I whispered.

By 5:15 pm, Divya's cervix fully opened. The hard crown of her baby's head moved steadily toward the light. Soon the urge to push overwhelmed her. Painful and powerful birth energy moved through her body. Divya cried. We held her up. Semi-reclining on the hospital bed, she curved around her belly. She transformed into an archetypal birth goddess, evoking primal power and strength. A new human being moved through her body. Between her legs, a new life descended. Divya fearlessly pushed for twenty-five minutes. Mercifully, her vagina opened fully and suffered no tear.

At 5:41 pm, I watched the midwife's experienced and competent hands catch a slippery, naked, and lovely little girl. The midwife and nurses joined us in celebrating another birth, fully extraordinary.

"Thank you, Lord!" Samuel exclaimed. They wept as their beautiful daughter was placed in Divya's welcoming arms.

Samuel cut the cord. "May God always bless you," he said. By 6 pm the room was clean, the bed made, and their new daughter was breastfeeding. I rubbed Divya's feet and watched the family rejoice in the everyday wonder of birth.

*

In doula work, yoga teaching, and mothering, a woman is called to love, nurture, soothe frayed nerves, and encourage the steady progress of nature. A year after Divya gave birth to her daughter, I discovered firsthand that motherhood is akin to doula work, except motherhood is a twenty-four-hour-a-day, seven-day-a-week adventure in giving. A loving mother nurtures an innocent life as it organically unfolds. A mother wisely guides, responds, and cares for her children so that their human potentiality can be realized. Yoga, life as a doula, and motherhood build upon each other. Each helped me to progress into full-hearted service, full-hearted giving.

However, a cardinal rule in giving is making time to receive; essential renewal time is vital. Professor of Psychology Carol Gilligan defines "mature care ethics" as embodying the balance of receiving and giving. According to Gilligan, women are conditioned to give, often at the expense of their own self-development. A mature approach to care honors the needs of self and other. Mirroring the pattern of each living breath, we need to inhale and receive care as well as exhale and give fully of our talents. In labor, contractions are followed by time for renewal. In motherhood, the early years of intense giving are followed by later years that hold more time for replenishing reflection.

All forms of birth—physical, intellectual, spiritual, and emotional—bring one to the depths. The power to give birth originates in the creative life spirit birthing all, the seen and the unseen. According to Joseph Campbell, the source of life is beyond gender and the duality of male and female. However, when symbolizing the power that creates, Campbell argues that the representation is "properly female." I agree. From this universal goddess energy emanates the seasons, the mountains, the rivers, and the galaxies. Writ large, human birth embodies the process of manifesting dreams, working diligently through our labors, and bringing vital energies to life. On this level, all humans give birth. All humans participate in life's creative energy.

On this level, we all need the renewing power of "rhythm, ritual, and rest." This phrase reminds doulas of three helpful labor techniques outlined by legendary doula trainer Penny Simkin. Rhythm, ritual, and rest not only aid birthing women, but they also support all of us to move skillfully through our life's labors. The power of rhythm restores vibrancy through dance, music, and motion. The power of ritual opens the way to a direct encounter with the mysterious wonder of life. Rest renews and restores the very cells of our often tired and over-stimulated bodies and minds.

Although I acknowledge the power of birth in its universal sense, as a doula I dive into the particular. Consider the power of a woman's body to give birth. The power of blood, sweat, and titanic challenge mixes with the labor of stretching, opening, and pushing. We all transitioned from a watery union with our mother's bodies to interdependent life on earth. All of us came through the body of a woman and whatever our relationship to this woman is today, this simple fact unites humanity. It also challenges us to create institutions dedicated to supporting the natural power of birthing and breastfeeding women.

A fierce dedication to the doula path informs my life. I've held the hands of women through cesarean deliveries, offered up my home as a safe place for laboring mothers in need of a location closer to the hospital, and even helped catch a baby when he arrived before the doctor did. The purpose behind providing this support is to ensure that the next generation receives the best possible start to life. A secure attachment bond with a healthy and loving mother or mother figure is indispensable.

Doulas work to ensure that the mother-child relationship gets off to the best possible start. The wellbeing of our human race is predicated upon such attachment. In *A General Theory of Love*, renowned professors of psychiatry Thomas Lewis, Fari Amani, and Richard Lannon reflect upon the biochemical roots of attachment and love located in the mammalian limbic brain. All nursing mammals are hormonally and intricately bonded with their young. Breastfeeding is evolution's wise way of sustaining the caregiving dance through the transfer of nature's most nutritiously dense food. The authors write that human children need "elaborate, individualized relationships with special, irreplaceable others." Without this deep investment of personalized care, limbic damage results. One may be cognitively gifted but emotionally bereft due to the loss of these primal and vital bonds.

Whether I'm teaching prenatal yoga to a Muslim mother pregnant with twins or closing my eyes in prayer as African-American Baptists petition the Lord for support during a difficult labor, the purpose of doula work inspires me to reflect upon the root of all ethical systems. Doulas offer a counterbalance to a medical system that places an inordinate amount of value on gadgets, medicine, and machines. Helpful and often lifesaving equipment need not eclipse the power of compassion.

Doulas are called to care, to encourage, and to leave the world better than we found it. Why not start where the world for each of us began? Why not begin with birth? Let us draw strength from birthing women who embody the goddess in her glory. Let us engage with our passions and birth our dreams. Let us meditate on the miracle of our own births. Let us honor the women who, through their very bodies, bestowed on us the gifts of life and life's companion gift, the mystery of death.

Chaplain

Clark and I sat in Lisa's cozy kitchen in Newport, Rhode Island. A lovely tapestry was draped over her dining room table. Her two cats scampered throughout the apartment as we laughed, enjoyed a glass of wine, and cleaned up after dinner. Then the conversation became serious. Lisa worked as an oncology nurse. She began to share stories about supporting patients through healing and dying. Intrigued, I came up with a thought experiment centered upon death's mystery.

If the answer to the ever-intriguing question about what happens after death were visible underneath Lisa's dining room table tapestry, would we look? To clarify, I explained that this vision would not include details about our own future deaths. Rather, we would perceive what happens after death for everyone. Was reincarnation true? Did consciousness dissolve as brain functioning ceased? Would we see that one religion reigned supreme in its theological proclamations concerning the afterlife? Would we encounter something that even in our wildest dreams we could not imagine? Would we tell anyone if we did look? Something indeed happens after we die. What would it mean to comprehend the truth about death?

We discussed and debated this for hours. Clark felt certain he would never look under the tapestry. His love for mystery and lack of fear of the unknown explained his reasoning. I wanted truth. Imagine actually apprehending this elusive, treasured, and so often feared unknown. Lisa could see both of our points of view and remained undecided.

What if one looked only to discover a horror? I trusted the love I've experienced in life enough to not fear this possibility. But would I really look? It's one thing to philosophize about aligning one's life with truth; it's quite another to purposefully confront its life-altering power. Throughout history, people have claimed to know the truth about the afterlife. They were deemed delusional or prophetic.

For years, I've used this "tapestry exercise" in my religion and philosophy classes. It never fails to provoke a powerful and at times difficult discussion. Becoming a doula transformed my teaching and my life. From the moment I heard about hospital chaplaincy, I knew a similar transformation was in store for me. As if it were alchemy, the training refined my very soul.

*

Much wisdom is found in clinical pastoral education (CPE). Chaplains practice holding open, loving, and holy space in the most difficult of times. Throughout my CPE training, the pluralistic, intellectually open, and progressive Unitarian Universalist tradition sustained me. I also drew on the solid bedrock foundation of my meditation and yoga practices. They provided immediately accessible centering techniques when coping with trauma. I needed all of the strength I could muster. I spent many long nights holding the hands of the sick and dying in a large, urban, New Jersey hospital.

We were an eclectic bunch. Presbyterians, Baptists, Catholics, evangelical Korean Protestants, and rabbis joined me for this journey. I was the only UU. Most of my fellow students were completing their CPE unit as a requirement for their future in church ministry. My goals were more personal. I wanted to experience the bookend of doula work. Knowing how powerful it had been to hold the hands of the birthing, I knew that much wisdom was to be gained from standing at the other end of life's threshold. One learns much about life by witnessing death.

Every Wednesday night, we gathered for a five-hour training session. Specialists from different hospital departments, such as the emergency room and oncology, visited and gave informative talks. Occasionally hospital chaplains witness joyful recoveries, but the majority of our work entails a direct encounter with life's repellent and frightening realities. Together, our group considered the following questions: What does it mean to enter a patient's room and be a compassionate witness to his or her pain? What does it mean to embody an open heart in the presence of great and unimaginable loss? What does it mean to die?

We spent many hours discussing the stages of grief and the process of dying, which provided ample material for sleepless nights' reflections. For nine months, we tried to befriend, or at least acknowledge, the fear that is death's companion. Author and teacher David Deida writes, "Almost everything you do, you do because you are afraid to die. And yet dying is exactly what you are doing, from the moment you are born." I had encountered this sentiment before during my time in India. According to the philosophy of Advaita Vedanta, all fear is rooted in *abhinivesh*, the fear of death. For example, we fear shame because it is a death to the ego. We fear aging because it is a death to our youth. In Buddhist teaching, all moments are born and die into each other. Leaving the womb is a death of one state of existence and a birth into another realm. Childhood dies into puberty and the elderly have experienced the death of their young adult years.

While I appreciated Deida's insights about our fear of death, his reflections on suffering moved me to tears. He writes, "You were born as a sacrifice. And either you can participate in this sacrifice, dissolving in the giving of your gift, or you can resist it, which is your suffering." So much of my own suffering resulted from resistance to the reality of life's impermanence. So much of the suffering I witnessed as a chaplain also directly connected to resistance. Of course, one fiercely resists accepting the premature death of beloved ones. I don't even want to imagine the pain of losing those closest to my heart to an early, tragic death. Yet chaplaincy training required me to do just this. I had to face my own resistance in order to offer a semblance of calm to heartsick hospital patients and their families.

Deida's teaching also offered vital ballast for my steady navigation through the rough waters of hospital chaplaincy. I am called to give my gifts. I was born to learn, serve, and dissolve into a deep love for the mystery that sustains me. In this sense, I was born as a sacrifice. I vowed to participate in this reality as bravely as possible.

We were each assigned a direct supervisor. The stars aligned and I considered myself lucky to be assigned to the only Quaker in the mix. I received extensive feedback and superb supervision. Weekly reports detailing encounters with patients were read aloud and processed as a group. We were asked to bring in the most difficult and challenging conversations to facilitate poignant personal growth. My supervisors and fellow classmates composed lengthy assessments of my interactions in class, in group process, and with patients. I did the same for them. Sometimes the feedback challenged my ego's pride. Sometimes the feedback opened the door of my heart, facilitating a deeper experience of compassion.

In many ways, our training was uncannily similar to group therapy. Until chaplains deal with their own grief, life traumas, and individual fears around death, they won't be able to clearly respond to the difficulties that hospital patients encounter. The danger is that we will project our personal issues and dramas onto those we are called to serve. For example, we risk walking into a hospital room and seeing our own ailing grandmother or grandfather rather than the person actually lying in the bed. Processing our own fears is a tonic that enables us to be of service. We can hold an open heart for others only to the extent that we are able to do so for ourselves.

I certainly didn't want my unresolved wounds to impede the work I felt called to do. I tried to take ownership of my projections and worked to remain open to critical feedback regarding my encounters with patients. Our supervisors warned us that chaplains can avoid being truly open while caring for those experiencing great pain. Even one's own religious tradition can be used as an emotional shield in this regard. We were taught to avoid prayer or spiritual talk that simply swept aside a patient's difficulties.

✿

Focus on empathy before meaning making.
Never mention God to a patient until you touch the pain.
If you don't have your feelings, your feelings will have you.

❊

CPE training made sense to me as a yoga teacher. The practice of mindfully breathing while holding a challenging asana gave me a good sense of what I was being called to do as a chaplain. The practice of holding space for a woman's pain during childbirth helped me listen compassionately to a dying man express wrenching regret for a life half-lived. My interest in dance, dreamwork, and body-centered therapies added depth to my hospital chaplaincy experience. At times, I meditated with patients during a chaplaincy visit. Once, I offered a woman a foot massage so she could calm down during a necessary medical exam. Focusing on the breath and the mindful use of therapeutic touch helped restore vital energies and relieve mental confusion.

Our CPE supervisors emphasized an archetypally feminine way of being. I often thought of the night sky, the moon, and a mother's gentleness while pulling an all-night shift at the hospital. It became important for me to walk out of the building and soak in the fresh air even for five minutes before continuing with my rounds. Our CPE supervisors encouraged us to listen more, care deeply, and soften around the hard edges of pain. The feminine powers of holding space and stopping to marvel at moonlight sustained me.

One day, our CPE director pounded his fist on the table, shouting, "You must be Feminine! Feminine!" The irony in his loud and stereotypically masculine gesture made me smile. From day one, I admired this heartfelt, cranky, and insightful man. It was an honor to spend nearly a year in a close supervisory relationship with him.

However, many of my peers felt that holding compassionate space and simply listening deemphasized their religious obligation to affirm beloved metaphysical teachings regarding truth. How could an evangelical chaplain hold the space for a dying atheist and resist the temptation to evangelize? How could we understand a patient's struggle rather than interpret it?

We spent many hours discussing the use of prayer. A few of my peers wanted to conclude their prayers with a proclamation of faith. They longed to end their pastoral visits by invoking the name of Jesus Christ, but when caring for a Jewish or Hindu patient, for example, this is not appropriate. Our director's wise reflections helped. He told the evangelicals in the group that although the hospital isn't a place for Christian chaplains to teach the word of Christ, it is a place for Christian chaplains to embody the Word. He advised us to set aside formulaic religious approaches and affirm love's essence. Regardless of a chaplain's religious or spiritual point of view, the chaplain must embody the spirit of compassion, which is known by many names. The patient's needs are primary. A patient's faith and identity must be honored. Some patients don't want to pray at all.

*

Simply sit vigil next to a person.
Place a hand on the back.

Have a listening heart.
That is enough.

*

Being compassionately open involves respecting one's limits. Reminded to "honor our edge," we were never asked to do something that went against our ethical or spiritual beliefs.

I met my edge one afternoon when I was called to the oncology floor. I sat by the bedside of a sixty-year-old woman in the last days of a disfiguring battle with cancer. Bald and barely conscious, she stirred and mumbled nonsense in a drug-induced state. She shook, quaked, and moaned. She smelled. Her eyes remained closed as I spoke softly to her. She didn't respond to my presence.

Her youngest son was also in the room. He had called for the chaplaincy visit. I focused my attention on him. "How can I best support you through this difficult time?" I asked.

He quickly explained that he had rejected his mother's Catholic faith and was a fundamentalist Foursquare Gospel Christian. He shifted nervously back and forth by her bed. "Do you have any anointed oil?" he asked. "Can you do an exorcism? My mother is possessed by demons. Yes, the demons have her."

"Demons?"

"Yes, she's clearly possessed."

At this point, I just stared at him. This was not what I had expected. I looked at his mother's bald head and gently touched her unmoving hand.

"What makes you think your mother is possessed?" I asked.

The young man described all of her physical symptoms. Again he asked if I would perform an exorcism. At this point, I had lost interest in having compassion and trying to understand his fears. I could no longer hold space for him. His focus on paranormal phantasies triggered my past. I quickly started to interpret what he was saying. My own harsh judgments began to arise.

"The symptoms you describe are the result of the pain medication your mother is taking. She is not possessed by demons," I said, trying to sound calm. I suggested he consult with the nurse regarding the normal responses to morphine. Inside, I saw my director's fist hit the table, as he demanded feminine energy to emerge. Yet how was I supposed to listen with openhearted compassion to this request for an exorcism? This appeal was for him, not her. How could I find a way to bring to light the nervousness, fear, and anxiety motivating him to seek out such a nightmarish response to his mother's impending death?

My worldview took center stage. I didn't want this woman "exorcised." She needed loving care, not fear-based, delusional mumbo-jumbo. My interpretive and judgmental thoughts rushed to the foreground of my consciousness. Surely one of my evangelical Christian colleagues could have handled this with greater understanding.

Finally, I said, "I simply can't do an exorcism for you. I don't believe in demons. I wouldn't even know how to pretend to do such a thing."

I've recited parts of *The Quran* with Muslim patients and invoked the Hail Mary prayer with Catholic patients. I've chanted sutras from *The Bhagavad Gita* with an elderly Hindu couple. Once I discussed whether the second law of thermo-dynamics applied to the energy of consciousness with a dying atheist professor of physics. I've brought Talmudic texts to rabbis facing death's threshold and prayed with strangers standing next to bodies in the morgue. But there was absolutely no way I could ever know where to start to even pretend to lead an exorcism. I had hit my edge.

I ended up leaving and later returned with prayer oil, which I gave to the son. I left again. While I was gone, a few of the son's friends from a local fundamentalist church arrived. I wasn't in the room for the dramatic showdown, but the nurses told me about the loud voices proclaiming the power of Christ who stands at the right hand of the Father. Finally, with Lucifer denounced, the room again was quiet. Only the sounds of beeping machines and an unconscious woman's breath remained.

Later, the patient's sisters arrived. As practicing Catholics, they expressed frustration with their renegade Foursquare Gospel nephew. The woman was dying. The sisters did what the son couldn't yet do. They mourned.

Within the hour, I sat with a different family in another hospital room and listened to the story of another illness and another passing. The hallways provided needed spaces for reflection. They were breathing spaces.

In all of my encounters, I wondered about my own understandings of birth, breath, and death. How could I stay open to these mysteries? I had practiced breathing mindfully in difficult places, including the loss of babies and the suicides of young men. It took great strength to hold space and breathe with them. I did my best to rely on a power greater than me to sustain me.

In one case, a dying man had traumatized his family so terribly that only one cousin showed up for his passing. She didn't even want to touch him. For two hours, I stood next to her and listened. The dying man was high on morphine and unconscious throughout. He could offer no healing words, no needed apologies. The cousin and I watched him die from gangrene of the groin. This seemed grossly karmic given the pain left in his wake, yet that is how he died.

In another case, an elderly woman had fallen off her porch while watering plants on a sunny afternoon. Bright red blood filled her mouth. While watching her breathe through this gaping wound, I was bewildered by the raw intensity of death's power. Her grief-stricken family gathered around her. We prayed together. She died in the ER.

In yet another case, a Polish woman had been hit by a white van while crossing the street. She was on her way to have coffee with her mother. Twelve hours later, doctors performed a gruesome but brilliant emergency medical procedure perfected on the battlefields of Iraq in which they temporarily put part of her skull inside her stomach. Her swelling brain needed room. By removing part of the skull and placing it in the stomach organ, the vital tissue stayed alive. After the swelling had gone down and the part of the skull replaced, her system didn't register it as foreign. It was a brilliant solution, but it frightened me.

Sometimes, I personalized these experiences. What if I were suddenly hit by a van and a part of my skull ended up in my stomach? I felt fear's ugly head rise up in my imagination. I took refuge in the practice of softening.

When I arrived for an on-call shift, I searched the hospital database for any UU patients in house. I loved visiting members of my liberal religious community. I sang "Spirit of Life" softly as I found my way to a UU patient's hospital room. This song, composed by Carolyn McDade, is sung weekly in Unitarian Universalist congregations around the world. I've turned to this song in times of personal crisis and in moments of pure gratitude. In particular, I love the ending: "Roots hold me close, wings set me free; Spirit of Life, come to me. Come to me." It was an honor to meet the needs and concerns of individuals within the expansive UU framework.

I also looked up any Mormons. LDS prayer language is encoded in my earliest memories of daily life. I could easily communicate with and serve those in the religious community who had nurtured me as a young girl. Praying to "Our Kind and Gracious Heavenly Father" still opens my heart. I've watched the men in my family gather around those in need of healing and offer up formal priesthood blessings with great love. To pray with Mormon patients in a large New Jersey hospital helped me honor my earliest memories of religious life that had formed me.

I've never been so extraordinarily grateful for my scholastic background in comparative religion and philosophy as I was during that time. As a chaplain, I competently drew upon the myths, symbols, and prayers of many faith traditions in my encounters with patients. To skillfully relieve even one patient's emotional burden with a prayer from his or her tradition was worth the years spent studying ancient texts. I humbly offered support to my peers who wanted to learn more about faiths outside of the Jewish and Christian traditions.

In particular, I was grateful to be an advocate for the Muslim patients I encountered. One time, I whispered, *"Allah uh Akbar"* over and over again into the ear of an Egyptian woman who had just survived a terrible car accident. The medical team couldn't get her to calm down and they desperately needed to stabilize her spine. I was called into the room. They may have been surprised by my approach. But it worked. "Allah u Akbar. Allah u Akbar." God is Greater. I found myself repeating this phrase for much of the day.

For me, this wisdom exists at the very heart of life. God is Greater. The Spirit of Life is Greater. The mystery at the heart of all things is greater than any theology, greater than any scripture, and certainly greater than my limited understanding.

When I was lucky, my chaplain's heart opened wide and allowed the waters of inspiration to wash through me. Patterns of significance and silence moved through my breath and body. The words would just come, allowing for grace, hope, and wholeness. Emily Dickinson wrote, "Not knowing when the dawn will come, I open every door." Much of my work as a chaplain involved having heartfelt patience for dawning light to lead me. Through my encounters with death, I became more open, daring, humble, and alive.

Would I look under the tapestry? What if the mystery present can only be loved, not understood? As choreographer Isadora Duncan once said, "If I could tell you what it meant, there would be no point in dancing it." Dancing was a tonic during my chaplaincy training. I'd often come home from a long shift at the hospital, close the drapes to the front room, turn up the music, and dance. Much of the pain and sadness carried home from the day moved through, and out of, my body. Dancing allowed me to deeply feel the difficult experiences without becoming overburdened by them.

*

I have many beautiful memories of the healing and uplifting power of dance. One in particular stands out. I close my eyes and see it so clearly.

I'm in New York City with Julie, a fellow teacher and my closest female friend. I am four months pregnant. After eleven years of working at The Lawrenceville School, Clark and I are preparing to move to Bogota, Colombia. We are excited about diving into the world of international teaching. To prepare for this momentous change, I want to soak in as much time with Julie as I can. I also want to surround my pregnant self with as much positive energy as possible.

Julie and I met in the summer of 2001 at a mosque in northern New Mexico. We both had signed up for a two-week immersion experience designed for educators who teach about Islam. When we weren't in class, Julie and I soaked in the radically gorgeous desert landscape. We hiked for hours, meditated, and shared many stories. We lost ourselves in laughter once when suddenly drenched by a tremendous desert rainstorm. I immediately was drawn to her open heart and loving, adventurous soul. She's also a yoga teacher who truly understands the power of dance.

In my memory, I see Julie and me enter into a large concert hall along with a thousand other yogis, mystics, and *kirtan* lovers. Kirtan, or call and response chanting, is one of our favorite spiritual practices. Known for her ethereal and healing voice, Snatam Kaur performs. The drums pick up. People everywhere are on their feet. An ecstatic dance erupts. Arms, hips, bellies, hands, feet, and hearts merge in vibrant, wild, holy abandon.

Snatam Kaur repeatedly chants, "Allah, Jehovah, Rama, Sa Ta Na Ma." For a seemingly endless amount of time, she sings the names of God honored in the Muslim, Christian, Hindu, and Sikh traditions. Together, we praise the power that holds, nourishes, and dissolves all life. She extends a prayerful blessing. A palpable feeling of yearning fills the room. A thousand voices join her. "Peace to all. Love to all. Life to all."

I'm the pregnant woman dancing. A little one is safely tucked inside my pink, pulsing womb. We are two sparks in this universal play of light and shadow. Images of the women I've supported as a doula, images of the patients I've cared for as a chaplain, memories of my family, all of this flows through me as I move. I dance for my beloved Clark. I dance for the wondrous child growing within me. I bow to all holy names. I honor the many paths that dear friends travel and remember the lessons of Jerusalem. Julie and I soak in the love found in this wondrous dancing tribe. I am home.

To be lovingly present through the primal, naked pain that marks aspects of birth, and to be lovingly present through the difficult, heart-wrenching ending that marks aspects of death is to learn about life and love. Fear may be strong, but love is stronger. Learning how to love includes learning how to make room for and transform fear. Learning how to live involves learning how to die. Love alone is the most potent power illuminating the breath's journey in between these thresholds. Love is the key. Love is the dance.

*

The body carries within its structure of all of one's life experiences. As a seasoned yoga teacher once told me, "The body is the scene of all our accidents." Injurious experiences are not only recorded in visible scars, but they also reside in the way we move, sleep, and unconsciously respond to stimuli. It is uncomfortable and painful to awaken to these patterns, but once we do, our awareness enables us to change them. A challenging death can open the heart. A difficult past can inspire a well-lived present.

The practice of yoga, or the healing power in dance, isn't about replacing darkness with light. It's about honoring both. In this context, darkness isn't evil. Rather, it refers to the undigested parts of the human psyche that catapult us into self-defeating and harming behaviors. The darkness of these fractured aspects within us only becomes evil when acted upon. When not brought into the light of wholeness, these fractured elements create history's infamous examples of hell on earth. When motivated by selfishness, resistance, revenge, or rage, we manifest mystery in a way that harms the very vehicles we have to perceive it. The body carries the energetic imprint of its wounding. As a chaplain, I could listen to people only to the extent that I had made peace with similar suffering inside of myself. Dancing freely, practicing yoga, and therapeutic healing modalities help me integrate life's light and darkness with honesty and love.

On the fourth floor of the Kripalu Center for Yoga and Health, I reflect upon the vital work of living an integrated life. Surrounded by hundreds of acres of beautiful land, Kripalu is America's largest yoga center. My heart leaps at the breathtaking vistas of the Berkshires, yet the fourth floor is my favorite place at Kripalu. Upon arrival, one's senses are filled with aromatic essential oils used in various healing modalities. Each year, tens of thousands of bodies and minds are touched, rested, and mended at Kripalu. Vital energy locked up in tension and pain is liberated.

What does it mean to heal? How do we breathe while healing? As I viscerally discovered in chaplaincy, healing isn't equivalent to curing. Healing may not even take physical pain away. However, key mental and emotional shifts provide even the dying with a healing breath of gratitude and compassion.

Many of Kripalu's healing arts practitioners come to their work after successfully navigating various life crises. In this way, they share journeys similar to those of the shamans of old. Joseph Campbell describes how ancient shamans were catapulted out of known realms of ordinary space and time, often by a severe illness or trauma. After facing arduous trials, they received luminous understanding. These ancient healers returned to their communities with curative gifts.

One summer afternoon at Kripalu, I signed up for a massage with a gifted therapist named Naomi. She had a healing gift. I rested on her massage table. Peaceful energy surrounded me. I enjoyed breathing deeply and feeling the release of the everyday surface tension held in the tissues of my body. At one point, she began to massage my face. As Naomi moved her hands over my jaw, memories of an old injury flooded my mind. Before this, all was placid and clear. Now a deeper healing opportunity opened and I had a choice. I could push memories aside and ask her to stop massaging my face, or I could see where it would lead me. I chose a deeper healing. I began to talk. I described the vivid imagery filling my consciousness. Naomi listened. I began to cry. Something opened. Once fractured and forgotten, a part of me surfaced. It wanted to be integrated.

I saw myself at five years old, a precocious little girl sitting at the top of the tallest slide at Greenwood Elementary School in American Fork, Utah. My sandal was stuck and I reached over to free my foot. I leaned too far, lost my balance, and fell. I watched my tiny form disappear into darkness. Later, in the hospital, I felt the pain of several knocked-out teeth and a severely broken jaw. My father was at work and our neighbor across the street helped my mother. My blood soaked through his shirt. My physical pain was compounded by complicated emotions. That day, I had worn my new sandals instead of the sneakers that my mother had wanted me to wear. She blamed herself for the fall and believed she wasn't "strong enough" to control me.

On the massage table, my consciousness occupied two places. I was receiving a massage at Kripalu and moving through an intense body memory that I had never processed. The energy surrounding this event had been locked in my jaw for twenty-six years. I continued to weep, and then, quite suddenly, the tears stopped and a renewing breath brought tranquility. My face tingled with aliveness. My jaw felt so different, even new. Over the next two days, I often paused to open my mouth and move my jaw around. Something had integrated. The tears I never cried as a child were free.

Nothing had felt repressed about my recollection of that fall. Before the massage, I had never felt compelled to dive into that specific memory. But the body is endowed with wisdom. Integrating the past frees us to be more fully alive in the present. Through emotional release and intellectual contextualization, we can reframe and in effect rewire our bodies and minds to be stronger. We need not carry around open and unattended wounds from long ago.

Consider the work of Dr. Joan Borysenko, famous for her vibrant contributions in mind and body healing as a professor of medicine at Harvard. Borysenko praises the pharmacological wonders found in Western medicine, yet she feels they are overused. She describes her own experiences of healing from chronic headaches, backaches, and panic attacks experienced while in the "rat race of overachieving." Drawing on integrating practices such as tai chi, yoga, and meditation, she recognized the clear connection between the negative images running through her mind and her physical stress.

Borysenko uses a Venn diagram showing three interlocking circles to symbolize our state of ease or disease. One circle represents genetics. Another stands for environment. The third represents willpower and the amalgam of past personal choices. According to Borysenko, all three circles are held within "the sacred mystery." The interplay of these four factors constitutes our state of happiness or health. Healing cannot be reduced to any one component alone. She firmly opposes the simplistic thinking behind "New Age guilt," which attributes all disease to conscious thought or willpower. A child does not "think" herself into leukemia, nor does an adult "manifest" a serious car accident.

Although we can't change our genetic inheritance, we can choose to bring out the best in our lives. We can learn about healing from modern psychological studies that focus on human happiness. All of us need healthy social connections, openness to new experiences, optimism, long-term loving relationships, meaningful work, and a cultivated sense of spirit and/or meaning. Meditation is an ancient and powerful technique that aids us along the way. Borysenko beautifully portrays meditation as "resting in the energy that holds you." She grew up in a Jewish home and meditation revealed to her that the "Holy of Holies" is within the heart, not in an ancient temple of long ago.

When the world seems too dismal for hope to be rekindled, I think of chaplaincy and I call Kripalu to mind. Every hour of every day, all throughout the year, a chaplain is on call doing rounds. That solitary figure walking the halls of a modern New Jersey level-one trauma hospital reminds me of the good in this world. Every day, people face their own vulnerabilities in Kripalu's sacred, safe, and healing space. Each mystical tradition also rekindles hope. There comes a point when the distinction between self and other is transcended by a vision of unity. Each faith is a direct and vibrant path leading adherents to the timeless source that upholds and sustains our world.

Drawing upon such hope, I continue to dance my prayer.

✳

May your goodness move through all. May your light move through all. From the very marrow of my body, I praise your grace. With gratitude for all that I can comprehend, I bow. Thank you, dear One known by a multitude of names yet ultimately beyond all embodied sound. May your kindness wash over my eyes so I can see clearly. May my mouth speak only truth, my mind be full of clear thinking, and my hands full of nurturing love. May this breath uplift me. May I hear your ancient rhythms.

Thank you for water, for nature, for the circular patterns of beauty found where rain meets the creek bed near our home. My son loves to stop on our walks and wonder at the water. Thank you beyond measure for this boy. I am so grateful I didn't miss motherhood. I'm so grateful for my son who laughs when the wind blows onto his tiny, new face. May your wind of kindness move through him and protect him all his days. With deepest gratitude, I acknowledge with joy that through me you gave birth to him. Give birth to my highest potential, God. Help me emerge as the person I am meant to be.

Thank you, breathing, dancing Jesus.

Taber

It took me a long time to heal my strong aversion to motherhood. For years, pregnancy and birth represented everything I had to avoid in order to create a life free of my mother's shadow. I needed years of journaling, therapy, and maternal mentoring to see myself as a mother. Together with dancing, yoga, and meditation, these healing modalities opened my once tentative heart. Marrying my husband, Clark, constituted the first step.

In 1996, our lives crossed outside of the Grand Canyon on a warm June day. Within the first hour of our meeting, I felt I recognized him. A deep part of me lived in him, and a parcel of his beautiful heart lived in me. It was simply a fact. We spent hours talking about philosophy and life. That night, I dreamt he lay on top of me, enveloping me with love's sweetness. Then light began moving out of his eyes into mine. "We can heal each other through our eyes," he said. These were the only words spoken in the dream. The light washed through my body and moved into my womb, setting my uterus radiantly aglow.

Looking back, I see how my dream was a premonition of our life together as lovers and parents. At the time, it surprised and embarrassed me. After all, I had just met the man. I later told Clark about the dream, initially leaving out the light in the uterus part. He questioned me and asked about a missing detail. Once we had fallen in love, he explained he had some-how known my dream.

The poet Oscar Wilde wrote, "It is love, not philosophy that is the true explanation of this world." I spent years run-ning from such a transformative love. Clark noticed right away and called me on it. Head over heels in love with this remark-able man, I decided I wouldn't run from him. Seventeen years later, I've stayed true to that promise.

Older female mentors offered more healing balm. Throughout my life, my father's sisters, my beloved aunts, were stalwart inspirations. When I was a girl, my Aunt Kris taught me how to ride a motorcycle and face my fear of drowning. She was my confidant when I navigated troubled waters and always enjoyed joining me for deep philosophical musings on life's purpose. My aunts lifted me up when my mother fell into her deep chasms of confusion. When my mother cut ties with four of her children, including me, my aunts were there to hold us in our pain. Inspired yoga teachers, kind-hearted therapists, and older female friends also mentored me through my adult years. I can't imagine my life without them.

Finally, I was ready. At the age of thirty-seven, I became pregnant. Nothing but joy filled my soul. The healing began.

My pregnancy lasted forty-one weeks and four days. Then our little one arrived and transformed everything with light. Through the birth of my first child and the subsequent opening of the deepest parts of my heart, I came to see that the balm for my pain entailed a loving return to the wounded place.

At first, the contractions were mild enough. I moved through my evening routine with joyful anticipation. Clark and I walked around a nearby neighborhood full of houses that reminded us of Mobile, Alabama, his hometown. We talked, dreamed, and laughed. When the contractions came, we fell into silence so I could practice slow deep breathing. I also squeezed his arm. By midnight, the contractions stopped. Already skilled at the art of practicing pregnancy patience, we went to bed.

I slept until 3 am. Then for some reason, I got up and meditated for an hour. It was a deep and peaceful place, a calm before the storm. I began to tire and fell asleep. At 4:30 am, I awoke from a vivid dream. In the dream, my uterus was a large, healthy, pink balloon contracting around a mysterious box. Somehow the box needed to be born and this soft, powerful organ could do it. The moment I recalled the details of the dream, my contractions started again. This time they did not stop.

The doorway to Labor Land opened. I knew full well that the birth experience soon would transform my very sense of time. At first, normal daily life routines are punctuated by ten-minute pauses. As the birthing mother's contractions intensify, she enters into a trancelike state. For six years prior to my pregnancy, I had served as a trusted confidant and guide for many women as they surrendered to this transformative process. Now it was my turn to cross the threshold.

Breakfast, artwork, rest, and a simple walk on a bright winter day filled our time. My contractions continued to intensify. By 3 pm, the women chosen to support us began to arrive. Clark referred to them as "the dream team."

Included in the mix were my sister Rachel and my doula Penny. Rachel and I forever treasure our memories of witnessing and holding sacred space for each other as we birthed our firstborn children. Penny was not only my doula; she was also my doula trainer, a massage therapist, and a dear friend. Her expertise and skill were unmatched. Six years earlier, she had taught and inspired me when I became a doula. Now she held my hand as I went into labor.

We hired extraordinarily gifted and down-to-earth midwives. Pam and Louise offered us holistic and no-nonsense support through their practice at Midwifery Care Associates. They specialized in homebirth and were well known as accomplished teachers of midwifery, often providing expert mentorship to midwives in training. One of their midwifery students, a gentle and quiet woman, joined us for the birth. Pam and Louise maintained full hospital privileges for patients who needed to, or preferred to, deliver in a fully equipped medical setting. I had known Pam and Louise for years before becoming pregnant. "If I ever have a baby, they are the women I want as my midwives." I told Clark. How grateful I was for their guidance throughout my pregnancy. They were the heart and soul of our dream team.

Throughout the afternoon, these loving women supported me with encouraging stories, laughter, touch, and empathy. The intensity of the contractions steadily increased and soon reached mind-altering crescendos. I couldn't help but move with them. I buried my head in Clark's chest and swayed and moaned. A wild woman slowly emerged inside me and began to rock my body with intensifying energy. My labor was coming on strong. It was not stopping and not slowing down.

At this point, my memory of the birth feels like a dream. I remember Pam saying I looked beautiful as I worked with the energy coursing through my body. I intuitively dropped to the floor, moaning or moving into various yoga poses. I let my arms dance and move at will. Primal sounds emerged effortlessly. We are undoubtedly mammals, animals, and creatures of this earth. Birth brought this truth home loud and clear. I remember entering the water. Clark had lovingly assembled a rented birthing tub in the kitchen. My descent into a profoundly deep and scary world accelerated and an unconscious power overtook me.

Even after my work as a doula, I had no idea how profoundly and utterly labor would unravel my world. Repeating positive phrases helped me make some space for the pain without interpreting it as suffering. I tried to compose myself and recited various phrases dozens of times. "It's prana. It's energy. It's light. It's the goddess," I softly said this over and over again.

An abundance of Kali energy arose during my arduous birthing experience. Kali, Hinduism's dark and fearsome goddess, is depicted with her bloody tongue hanging out of her mouth. She wears a necklace made of severed heads. The word "Kal" means "time," and Kali represents the inevitable end of the body's existence, ignorance, and ego-centered living. One must surrender everything and walk through the fearsome doorway leading to her grace. Kali is revered and beloved as a sacred mother goddess. When she ends our ignorance, she bestows the beatific vision of truth on us. During my birthing experience, Kali moved through me and cracked open any hesitation to fully express the overwhelming sensations coursing through my body.

Finally, I stood up, pulsing, pregnant, and dripping with water. Someone wrapped me in a dark purple towel. Clark and I went into the back bedroom alone. I moved, cried, and prayed.

Pressing my head into Clark's chest and holding onto his neck for support, I swayed to and fro in a wide-legged stance. I surprised myself with the sheer volume of prayers that punctuated my labor. Multifaith petitions for strength and relief effortlessly fell from my lips. "Help Me God!" "Kali, please!" "Jesus, give me strength!" Once, I heard myself roar. My hair was a matted mess.

Clark and I rested together in the uncannily calm moments between these storms. My husband never left my side. Sometimes we even looked at each other and laughed. The light from his eyes entered mine and sustained me. He never judged. He held me with profound love, a gift beyond measure. He was my love. My rock.

Around 6 pm, I asked my midwife to check my cervix. It had opened to seven centimeters -- wonderful news. Yes, I could do this. Rejuvenated, I surrendered to the ebb and flow of pain and rest. Around 9 pm, I slowly made it back to the birthing tub. My dream team was fully assembled. Yogic sounding really helped. My "Oh!" morphed into "Om." Clark harmonized with my voice and soon the whole group held a continuous "Om" that guided me through the contractions. The pain moved more easily encircled by the primordial water and sound.

And then everything stopped. I reached another resting phase, during which a softening calm descended. Intuitively, we all meditated together. The contractions paused. Was I entering the second stage of labor, the pushing stage? I felt pressure building between my legs. Pam encouraged me to "push into it a bit." So I did. But she needed to make sure my cervix truly was ten centimeters before I pushed fully.

The moment of truth occurred around 10 pm. My cervix was still at seven centimeters. My God. The contractions returned with a tremendous force. At that point, I entered into the archetypal "dark night of the soul." I've never fallen so deeply inside a cave of pain. My lower back blazed. It felt like it was on fire. I felt crazy, beyond-words, intense flames of painful fire. Time collapsed in on itself and morphed into excruciating moments punctuated by what seemed to be mere seconds of rest. Like a dying fish, I flopped and flipped in the birthing tub. I began to panic. While surrounded by compassion, I saw looks of concern pass between the members of my support team. I was scared.

My ultimate goal for the birth was to make sure my heart didn't shut down. In the face of intense fear or pain, I can become numb. It's a legacy drawn from my mother's emotional makeup. For years, she rarely expressed vulnerability. Cold, quiet, distant, and ominous energy surrounded her. Given this, I longed to remain connected to my heart, to embrace my vulnerability, and make room for all emotions that may arise. I needed to be present for this momentous birth.

At first, all I had to do was look at the love surrounding me. Everyone encouraged me to stay the course. Even though the time between contractions was minimal, I heard Penny say, "All is well. All is well." I looked at her and nodded in agreement. Then I was swiftly pulled back into the depths. For the next two hours, I gave my homebirth my all.

At midnight, I asked the midwife to check my cervix again.

Nothing had changed.

My heart was so heavy and my body was simply exhausted. The pain was relentless. I began to suffer.

Drawing upon my doula training and basic self-preservation, I knew I needed to go to the hospital to get medical relief. Pam suggested that Clark and I discuss transferring to the hospital by ourselves. I didn't want a discussion. I didn't want to labor in that house for one more minute.

Clark gently reminded me of my desire for a homebirth. He knew I didn't want to succumb to unnecessary medical interventions that are sadly too common in American hospitals. According to the World Health Organization, the "best outcomes for women and babies appear to occur with cesarean section rates of 5% to 10%." In the US, due to malpractice litigation, fear of vaginal delivery, and an overreliance on a mechanized vision of birth, the cesarean rate is 33 percent. I had no intention of delivering my child through major abdominal surgery unless it was truly medically necessary. Ideally, I wanted to have this beloved child at home. Yet I absolutely knew that I needed to go to the hospital. Pam and Louise would continue my care. They maintained a cesarean rate of less than 4 percent and approached their practice of midwifery as a true vocation. I knew they were committed to providing me with their very best. I trusted them implicitly.

With steady words, I said, "I don't want to be traumatized by this birth, Clark." Without missing a beat, he got on board and took care of the logistics.

The trip was treacherous and my outfit comical. I wore no underwear, bra, or socks. I did throw on a large "Stop Global Warming" bamboo t-shirt. Because I was bleeding, I put an extra-large absorbent pad between my legs. It stayed precariously in place with the help of a pair of randomly selected shorts. Someone assisted me in slipping on my grey and white sneakers, tying my laces in record time. With determination, I made it down the stairs. Barely pausing to notice the cold night air, I quickly opened the door to our black Volkswagen Jetta. The pressure and pain made sitting impossible, so I knelt in the front passenger seat and turned to face the rear of the car. I continued to sway, rock, and cry as Clark carefully navigated the New Jersey back roads that were populated with deer. I held onto the headrest for dear life.

Pam rode with us. She thought I might very well deliver on the way. In between the contractions, she reminded me of the reality awaiting me at the hospital. I would need to be admitted and get an IV drip going before I'd experience any medically induced reprieve from the pain of this difficult labor. "I just want you to know that relief won't happen right away," she said. It was also possible that my cervix would open in transit. Pam let her position be known if I was ten centimeters dilated upon arrival to the hospital, "I'm not going to drug you or the baby. You can push this baby out, Amy." I knew she was completely right and tried to focus on her rationally presented plan.

We arrived at the main hospital entrance. Pam quickly got out of the car and brought me a wheelchair. While Clark parked, she rapidly pushed me through the long hospital hallways to the labor and delivery area. It was a quiet night for the staff. Our midnight arrival was met with skilled and rapid assistance. We were assigned a room. I remember the slight sting of the blessed IV being placed in my left hand. I knelt upright on the hospital birthing bed and continued my prayerful rocking. I remember saying, "I want a full dose." Then I got very sleepy.

Unfortunately, the administered drug, Nubain, did not take the pain away. As one of my doula friends later told me, "Just call Nubain 'no brain' and you'll be closer to the truth." The drug simply zonked me out cold between contractions. I awoke with each one, startled, scared, and hurting. Clark was the only one who could do anything that brought a semblance of consolation. My dark night of the soul was suddenly high on a mind-warping narcotic. I was a sorry sight to behold.

At 2 am, my cervix remained open at seven centimeters.

At this point, Pam took charge. "Amy, you are going to have an epidural and you are going to rest." She ordered the epidural, a rare call for her in her midwifery practice. Epidurals are used by less than 5 percent of their birthing moms. My brilliant team of midwives made wise choices about my care and significantly increased my odds of having a vaginal birth. Although they were not fans of using an epidural, they remained open to it. Never doubting the power of my body, they reassured me that I had the strength to complete this difficult birth. Due to their unfailing support, I did not return to that earlier place of suffering.

The anesthesiologist gave me a strong initial dose of medication through the epidural. I remember painlessly receiving a catheter. The room became quiet. The nurse turned off the lights. Louise soon came to the hospital to take over and give Pam and their midwifery student a needed rest. Rachel and Penny slept the best they could in moderately comfortable hospital chairs. Sitting at the foot of my bed, Clark laid his head on my feet. "I love you, Amy," he said. My precious devoted husband closed his eyes.

Louise encouraged me to rest fully until I felt a very strong urge to push. "Let your body do the work. You need to sleep," she said. I felt nothing and fell into a peaceful emptiness.

After the birth, I learned the baby's head was asynclitic, meaning tipped to one shoulder. This awkward head-to-pelvis positioning produces very long and painful labors. Often there are few pauses between contractions.

Once the wild ride had stopped, the baby's head turned, and my body opened. My body wanted to open. My little one wanted to be born. My soul touched a deep place of silence. I experienced the simple, quiet space of slumber. Despite the treacherous eight-hour ordeal at seven centimeters dilated, I awakened with new energy.

When the sun rose the next morning, I was fully open at ten centimeters. Louise again advised me to keep resting until I felt the pressure to push. So I did. A few more hours passed. Then I felt the pressure. It was unmistakable. It was time.

At first, I agreed to push only reluctantly. It all seemed so surreal. I was hooked up to all sorts of beeping machines, trying to wrap my mind around the magnitude of what I had just experienced. With Clark's help, I decided to trust the process again. I decided to push. Remarkably and gratefully, pushing initiated a positive feedback loop. With each push, my will increased. With each push, I became more and more determined. By 10:30 am, I earnestly pushed. My loyal, sleep-deprived companions surrounded me. Our excitement increased. "That's it, Amy! You can do it." Their voices of encouragement mixed with my extraordinary effort.

Pushing hard, I felt sweat pour down my face. My gifted doula helped me curl around the baby. Although I tried different positions, most of the time I pushed while reclined on my back, legs wide open, knees bent, feet to the sky. In yoga, it's called happy baby pose. I actually thought of that at one point. It made me smile: happy baby's pose. I repeated the positive phrases that sustained me earlier in labor. "It's prana. It's energy. It's light. It's the goddess."

In Spanish, to give birth translates as *dar a luz,* meaning to be born into light. While pushing, I focused on a bright ceiling light and repeated this phrase, too. "Dar a luz, Amy. Dar a luz."

At one point, I wondered if our baby was a boy or a girl. Long before I was ready to conceive, Clark and I had picked out our favorite names. Why not? Who knows what the future might bring? Years later, when I did get pregnant, we decided not to find out the sex of our baby and let it be a surprise. Was this child Maline or Taber? I wondered and pushed again. I drew upon the strength of the women I had once helped through labor. I reminded myself that I'd seen it done. I knew the vagina could open without injury.

I never worked harder for anything in my life.

I felt something very large move. It clearly was not my body. Then, it happened. Another human body slipped out of my own. As the skull of my baby's head parted the tissues that had protected and sustained life in utero, the hard shell of my wounded heart irreversibly cracked open. Light poured in.

On Wednesday, December 7, 2011 at 11:45 am, our baby entered this world. Shaking and in shock, I heard my precious child cry. Clark collapsed in my arms with the news. Tears poured down his cheeks. He said, "It's Taber! Amy, it's Taber!" Our son. We wept with joy.

Taber's birth remains the most visceral and vivid experience of my life. "Without a skid mark," as Louise put it, my body opened without injury. The power of birth coursed through every cell of my being. Placed on my chest, Taber's naked, newly born body melted my heart. I felt intense and immeasurable love. Clark and I marveled at the very embodiment of our love, our miraculous son. We were surrounded by a love the depths of which I could not fathom but which was nonetheless real.

Deep, whole, and wise, Taber's eyes were his most striking physical feature. The epitome of innocence, he looked at me with pristine wonder and the purest love. We gazed at each other in timeless admiration. I can't even write this without crying. No one had looked at me like that before, and no one could. To paraphrase a beloved saying about motherhood, only a child knows what his mother's heartbeat sounds like from the inside. This little person literally had lived inside of me. God looked into my very soul through Taber's eyes.

Taber knew me as his mother and he was my son. What is it like for a newborn to see a human face? After perceiving only the subtlest play of light and shadow within the womb, he suddenly was able to see. Having heard my voice for months, Taber could now behold my form. My loving eyes welcomed him fully to this world. I fell completely in love with my boy. For three hours, we bonded skin to skin. For three hours, no routine tests were done. We simply bathed in the sight, smell, and touch of each other.

Clark held his son. My husband's strong loving arms gently cradled this little miracle. I watched Clark with awe. For so many years, he was beyond patient with my inner wrestling.

Did I want to be a mother? Due to my past, I had felt ambiguity, fear, and negativity, which distorted my vision. Clark loved me throughout, so much so that at one point, he set aside his lifelong dream of fatherhood to remain committed to our love. With a combination of resolve and grace, I came through the confusion. Love's clarity reigned. I marveled at the sight of these two amazing souls getting to know each other. "You won the daddy lottery," I tell Taber today. It's true.

Taber didn't cry once he rested in our arms. Even now, his energy remains peaceful, happy, and gentle. He's also a handsome boy. He has his father's good looks. According to Clark, he has my eyes.

What does it mean to dar a luz, to be born into light? For the sun, the task appears effortless. The moon takes a twenty-eight-day journey. For infants, they literally move from the fertile darkness of their mother's bodies into an illuminated world full of human potential. For me, birthing was a crucible moment, a dying, a deepening, and a healing. The light of birth transformed me into a mother. The light of birth is love. Looking back, I see this clearly. Love was the pain and joy. Love restored me as I rested and held me up when I transformed into a wild-eyed Kali. Love chanted with me in the birthing tub and love was certainly the epidural. Love pushed my baby out and gazed at me through Taber's eyes. Love sustains me now as I watch his sweet small mouth suckle my breast.

Love stopped the running.

Suddenly everything was clear. The radiant vividness of loving Taber, Clark, and creation transformed everything around me into radical beauty. Within hours of Taber's birth, I was humbled by the immensity of love pouring forth in all directions. I turned to Clark and said, "I am so grateful I didn't miss this." I cried joyful, gracious, and merciful tears.

While I never received a word of congratulations from my mother, soon after the birth, Aunt Kris flew across the country to nurture us and celebrate. She provided healing and holy company, mending my soul.

*

I never felt closer to spirit. Despite postpartum bleeding and initially sore nipples, I lived in a constant state of meditation, baby bliss, and motherly love for the first six weeks of Taber's life. Breastfeeding, waking at all hours to marvel at wonder incarnate, and crying healing tears filled each precious day. Transfixed by the magnitude of what I had just experienced, I vowed never to forget the miracle of this boy's birth. I prayed for my heart to expand with the knowledge that holy wonder surrounds every human birth. If such love guided our politics, no one would launch a war. Who would drop a bomb where innocent little ones nurse, sleep, and trust us to love them?

Throughout my pregnancy, I imagined I could continue to live the professional life I'd always known, with only slight modifications due to the addition of mothering. After Taber's birth, this completely changed. I literally dreaded even the thought of returning to work. Whenever I contemplated it, I cried. It felt so deeply and instinctively wrong. All I longed to do was nurture this boy.

It would take six months for Clark and me to radically shift our plan. For the time being, I needed to return to work to maintain our financial stability. I was on maternity leave when I had Taber in New Jersey, but we were living in Bogota, Colombia. I taught philosophy and ethics at a remarkable bilingual school. Surrounded by gifted and kind colleagues, I truly loved working abroad. Clark and I fully affirm the transformative power found in international travel and we embraced the challenge of becoming new parents in a foreign country. How could I have anticipated my profound change of heart? Returning to Colombia to finish the academic year would be the hardest six months of my life.

I remain forever indebted to the visionary, elegant, and loving director of my school in Colombia. She had stayed home with her own children when they were small and understood the depth of a mother's attachment. She certainly worried about the difficulty of my situation. I was a new mother in a foreign land and my heart was breaking. She changed the rules of the school's *guadaria*, or day care. Previously, only babies older than six months could be cared for on campus. Now, I was able to bring Taber with me to work. So twice daily, Taber and I navigated the frightfully congested freeways of Bogota together. He stayed in the guadaria while I taught my classes. I nursed, sang, and soaked in time with him in the interim. Often, I simply took him to my classroom with me. He slept in his sling while I lectured on Plato. My students adored him. I was surrounded by extraordinary kindness and love. The woman who ran the guadaria became a confidant. She wiped away quite a few of my tears. Yet even with baby in tow, work felt like a prison sentence. I counted the days leading to our return home.

Taber needed me. There would always be high school students to inspire and teach. But there was one Taber, and he had one mother. When we were apart, Taber often remained inconsolable and frequently cried himself into a shaky, exhausted sleep. The memories of returning to him after teaching, his eyes swollen with sadness, still haunt me. I lost all desire to do anything but respond to the biological fact of the mother-child attachment. Millions of years of female mammalian biology profoundly transformed my biochemical makeup. A mother bear awoke within me. Attachment isn't for the fainthearted and I've never been fainthearted.

The dependency characterizing the early years of the mother-child relationship has wisely evolved. This relationship links all generations. Quoting from *The General Theory of Love*, "An organic capacity for self-directedness" exists in all children. The independence so highly valued in Western cultures "emerges naturally not from frustrating and discouraging dependence, but from satiating dependence." The tether that connects mothers and children is a holy of holies worthy of society's utmost protection. For mammals, the care and attachment associated with breastfeeding fuels the healthy development of the limbic brain associated with the capacity for empathy and love. For me, it is impossible to imagine that anyone else should spend the day caring, nursing, and loving my baby boy.

If I could travel back in time and give sage advice to my strong-willed, free-spirited, pregnant self, I'd say the following:

Let motherhood work her wise ancient magic on you. Soon, you'll hold your son. Nothing in this world will mean more to you than to treasure the early years of breastfeeding and nurturing. Already fulfilled with a satisfying and happy career, you will long to let it go and move into your mothering years with a joy you can't fathom. It will take some time to rearrange the details, but your stay-at-home status is around the corner. Gather up the light within and trust it to guide you through this difficult detour. For the first time in your life, a hidden, soft, sweet space in your heart will open fully. You've never loved like this. You will love this little one beyond words.

*

Today, I snuggle with my growing one-year-old wonder as he takes to my breast. We sit in a cozy armchair where I learned to nurse him. Hours of sweet, warm, milk-giving kindness are woven into its very fabric. The familiar checkered pattern provides a steady background to the marvelous growth I see in Taber's feet, face, and hands.

My son begins to doze and I close my eyes. We are surrounded by a silent, life-giving peace. I open my eyes and look at the kitchen, the wooden cupboards, the gas stove, and the square dining table. Last year, a large birthing tub rested on the floor, and my laboring heart gave its all there. My beloved Aunt Kris placed delicious homemade meals on that very table. Together we celebrated my freshly triumphant passage through the threshold of motherhood. We celebrated the fires of transformation wherein I faced my fears.

Two Bullets

He arrived dead. The police found his body on a curb between the road and the sidewalk, which served as the killer's dumping ground. Certainly a name and a story accompanied this lifeless body lying on the hospital bed, but neither the hospital staff nor the police knew anything about his biography. Technologically advanced lifesaving machines remained unusually silent in the trauma bay. Two police officers stood guard at the entrance to the emergency room. My chaplaincy badge granted me entrance. The heavy doors swung open and the officers moved aside. I took a deep breath.

A male hospital technician waved me into the room and said, "Go do your thing, Chaplain."

I saw the wounds up close. Two bullets had entered his back and come out of his chest above his left nipple. Who shot these bullets? The police referred to the murder technique as "execution style." A doctor, who was visibly moved by this stranger's sudden death, simply called the murder "senseless." Indeed. What sense is there in such cold aggression in which form and substance were violently torn asunder?

I had never seen a murdered body. My heart pounded. During my twenty minutes with him, he remained an unknown man estimated to be in his thirties.

A solemn nurse washed bloodstains off the man's face. After being shot, he had fallen facedown on the road. "His face got banged up," she explained. Her hands shook as she washed him. Had he been robbed? He lacked all forms of identification and wore no jewelry.

Whenever I think about the terrifying toll of human violence exacted on each generation, I think of that man. In movies, countless bodies are shot and killed for entertainment, but there is nothing entertaining about such incidents. Was this violent end his karmic lot or a painful example of free will gone askew? Is there a creator God that knew this was going to happen? Is there a supernatural sinister sickness at work that moves people to murder? I wondered about human violence, mostly done by men to men.

To stand in front of a murdered man and be called to offer consolation is deep and difficult work. I imagined his body as a newborn boy. A mother marveled at every inch of it with precious tenderness. Why had he been shot through the back? Was he a father? A husband? Certainly he was a son to parents somewhere who tragically didn't know that it was time to grieve.

The nurse finished washing his face. I placed my hand on his exposed bare chest, which was cold to the touch. Would he be all right with this gesture of human kindness? How would I want my body treated after such a brutal assault? What if he had been my husband? My brother? Taber? I consciously and prayerfully worked to calm my overactive, scared, and discursive mind.

"May the wisdom of compassionate silence fill me," I prayed.

It was nighttime. The stars were out. Far above the fluorescent hospital lights, timeless, deep, dark space softly held our spinning world. I closed my eyes. The depth of the sunless, womblike sky filled my awareness. An immense spaciousness surrounded our planet, our solar system, and all galaxies. We were spinning in quiet, empty peace. It held all, including the realities of birth and death. This space held that man's story. I didn't need to know the details of it in order to touch him with kindness. I breathed in and prayed. Finally, my mind was quiet.

Gentle words came to me. I softly honored his life, and together with the nurse, we grieved his unexpected and traumatic passing. Tears poured from my eyes as I fully took in the sight of pierced skin. Bullet holes penetrated all the way through his chest. I kept my hand on his chest, a living hand on a still heart. The nurse and I stood together and acknowledged the life force that had once animated his form. I have never forgotten this man.

✼

I turn to the wisdom of ages for sound advice in my efforts to diminish human suffering. In *The Analects*, a student asks Confucius, "Is there any single word that could guide one's entire life?" Many good answers to this student's question exist. Love is a wise teacher and a wise guide. So is truth. Yet Confucius invokes the power of mutuality when offering his response: "Should it not be reciprocity? What you do not wish for yourself, do not do to others." Who would wish to be the man killed by two bullets?

Is there one word that can guide us in life? This is an important question. Sailors throughout the ages have looked to the stars to guide their wooden boats home. Arab astronomers invented the astrolabe in an attempt to outline their place in the universe. Birds of flight navigate by stars and avoid winds that could take them off course.

Connecting to the life around us and coming to care for its wellbeing constitute difficult and deep work. Compassion underlies reciprocity. As Plato said, "Be kind. For everyone you meet is fighting a hard battle." We are called to love, listen, and wish for each other what we wish for ourselves. Whether a chaplain, a nurse, or a man with a gun, we need to pause and consider reciprocity. No one wants to be shot in the chest and found utterly alone on a curbside. When we disrespect each other, we ignore the inescapable network of life's interdependence and create unnecessary pain in the world. People who practice gratitude and nurture a vision of connection don't add to such pain. Rather, they work to study, change, and transform it.

Humans tell stories to aid each other in the pursuit of discerning wisdom. In its truest sense, education makes vibrant interdisciplinary connections that inspire meaningful action to benefit our world. As a teacher of ethics, I felt a strong obligation to instruct in such a way that strengthened the cycle of reciprocity upon which the human family depends. Often stories from my hospital chaplaincy days served as powerful real-life lessons in ethics. To me, true education is rooted in the values of living honestly, loving fully, and contributing to the good in our world.

The gifted teachers I have known used carefully crafted imagery and stories to enact meaningful change with the hope of reducing human suffering. For example, Professor of Philosophy Peter Singer uses a simple story to provoke meaningful action to end world poverty. He asks his students to imagine walking by a pond on their way to work and to notice a small child fighting for his life in the water. The child can't swim and without assistance is surely doomed. Singer asks his students to imagine they are wearing a very expensive pair of shoes. Rushing into the water and saving the child will ruin this prized possession. Who would choose his or her shoes over the life of a helpless drowning child? No one should. Singer goes on to equate the pond with world poverty. Children everywhere are drowning in abject destitution. For the price of a single pair of expensive shoes, a life could be saved. This type of storytelling can be transformative and move a generation of inspired youth to action.

I often think of the mother of that unknown murdered man. I close my eyes and imagine the tears a mother sheds upon learning that her child had been murdered. What of the mothers who daily witness their children succumb to the cruel fate of abject poverty? I reflect upon Singer's powerful teaching metaphor. As a mother, I would kiss the feet of anyone who saved my drowning son.

I work to transform the pain of that experience into motivation for meaningful action. When the great mystery of death is upon me, I pray I leave this world a better place than it would have been if I had never lived at all.

*

Sitting on the floor of London's busy Heathrow Airport, I awaited my boarding call and passed the time writing in my journal. I can see myself clearly. I was a young twenty-year-old college student, but I can't remember if I was on my way to India or on my way home. I can recall his bright red cowboy boots. I certainly remember his strange scary words. Surrounded by international travelers, flight announcements, and my backpack, I saw him walk by, notice me, and suddenly stop. He was older, tall, and dark skinned. His shiny red boots interrupted my writing and his stern dire warnings captured my attention: "You, young lady, you'd better watch out."

"Excuse me, sir?" I asked.

"I'm telling you, watch out," he said. "There are dangerous strangers around here. They pretend to befriend young girls like you. They'll offer to take you out to dinner, and when you aren't looking, they'll slip drugs in your drink. You'll be kidnapped, raped repeatedly, and then sold underground as a prostitute."

I looked at him, surprised by his boldness and shocked by such brutal imagery.

"I'm warning you!" he said and briskly continued on his way.

The man's nightmarish injunction could serve as the script for a movie about human trafficking. Clearly he thought he was doing me a favor. As a twenty-year-old woman traveling alone, I should have paid more attention to the news regarding the horrifying world of modern-day slavery. Instead, my focus was on meditation, reading, and philosophy. All I thought about was saving enough money to return to the Himalayan meditation center in India.

A decade later, I encountered the work of Canadian journalist Victor Malarek, who spent months investigating the underbelly of human trafficking. Previously, Malarek had worked as a war correspondent. The brutality of modern slavery haunted him more than war. Tragically, every year, tens of thousands of unsuspecting, young, and vulnerable women and girls are sold into sexual bondage.

While reading Malarek, I remembered the strange man in red cowboy boots from my traveling days in India. Life energy, breath energy, also fuels this multibillion dollar trade of pain. How to explain this? Is breath morally neutral? Is mindfulness of breath able to facilitate the cruel power of lost and heartless men? Zen master Thich Nhat Hanh states, "In mindfulness, compassion, irritation, mustard green plant, and teapot are all sacred." The rosebush comes from the same seed and includes both thorns and petals. Therefore, the source and the manifestation are all filled with the same energy of life. Even cruel and violent people carry sacred life energy. They tragically choose to use their power to harm it.

According to Professor of Psychology Jonathan Haidt, ethics originates in the need for tribes to cohere. Given that genetics and culture "co-evolve," ethical precepts guiding human behavior are hardwired in the brain's structure itself. It's true that common moral impulses express themselves differently in each culture, but just as the human body needs Vitamin D in order to sustain healthy immune function, a human society needs an ethical code in order not to dissolve into chaos. We live in a post-tribal, globally interconnected age. May we honor our diversity even while fostering and affirming cross-cultural ethical precepts.

I again draw upon Ken Wilber's deep and surface structure framework. Ethical behavior clearly constitutes a deep structure. It doesn't depend on a shared metaphysics. One need not affirm the existence of a mutually accessible ultimate truth in order to act humanely toward one's fellow human beings. Whether a Muslim friend regards my daily meditation practice as leading me to the same place as her morning *fajr* prayer matters little to me. I'm not interested in whose path is more valid, whose scripture is more divinely inspired, or whose guru or prophet is more awake. I'm much more invested in how my friend and I actually treat each other. People don't have to agree about the mystery of truth in order not to kill each other.

Philosophical and religious traditions articulate similar ethical visions aimed at guiding interpersonal behavior. Even if only upheld for an inner circle of believers, humility, honesty, loving kindness, justice, and compassion are celebrated values. For the religiously observant, ethics are an inherent part of living in accord with a divine order. Do ethics actually come from a supernatural being or source? It doesn't matter. We can debate their philosophical origins and, as a scholar of religion and philosophy, I find it fascinating to do so. However, what matters in the end is their observance. When they are lived, ethical precepts build bridges, heal hurts, strengthen communities, and nurture healthy families. They offer heart medicine to an ailing world.

Through spiritual practice, the energies of aggression and cruelty eventually succumb to the power of mindfulness. Allowed to flow, the broad and expansive power of mindful breathing organically calms inner confusion and moves us to healing waters. I take refuge in this truth. Consider the well-documented experiences of incarcerated prisoners practicing *vipassana*, a Buddhist breath-focused meditation practice. If breath were indeed morally neutral, then eight days of silence focusing on the breath would not result in changes to the egos at hand. Yet those who choose silence and practice the ancient art of breath awareness emerge transformed. They do. I have.

Why? The power to see clearly into the moment frees us from habitually responding to aggression with more force. No matter what is going on, mindfulness and compassion can be cultivated and practiced even in the midst of negative and painful feelings. Mindfulness of life's unifying energy inspires the protection of life and enables us to act in a way that does not perpetuate ignorance or suffering. Our collective future depends on how people everywhere manifest love or hate.

✻

Sit up. Relax your shoulders. Soften the muscles around your mouth. Watch the mind without judgment. Gently place your attention upon the breath. Over time, this will reveal the source of attention itself as a holy mystery worthy of respect.

Let multiple thoughts arise and go. Do the same for any physical sensations that arise. If you become uncomfortable, gently adjust your seat. If the mind is really busy, use a mantra or prayer to calm the drama.

Close your eyes and watch the space within. Let it serve as a constant reminder of the infinite space that holds all the manifestation, which is ever open and loving. May this energy inspire all to honor life and work to end systems of oppression. May mindfulness of pain inspire a heart committed to love in the face of pain.

✻

Psychologist Daniel Goleman outlines numerous systems of meditation. After a thorough examination of a wide variety of meditation traditions, he notes the clear consistency in the way that higher states of awareness are described. Different names are utilized to describe the energy of mindfulness, but the power, state, and pure awareness that transform a human being are universally experienced.

How I wish to breathe peace and courage into the shaking limbs of every enslaved woman and girl. How I wish their captors and johns would awaken to their capacity for compassion. The man in the cowboy boots warned me of the negative powers of an unmindful and disconnected human mind. Compassionate mindfulness is the antidote.

As a chaplain, I encountered the harm caused by the shockingly ignorant brutality of human cruelty. Many times, I could respond only with loving silence and a few gentle words. I chose to place the difficult questions surrounding such cruelty at the feet of the silent space within and around me. Peace resides in the courageous calm found in the midst of a difficult storm. I find peace when I remember the nurse's skilled, shaking hands. I find peace when holding the innocent, sweet body of my sleeping son.

The misuse of those two bullets reminds me to enter into a silent power greater than the mind. When I enter that silence, that vast space within, it offers a peace stronger than human cruelty. May this peace offer sustenance as we hold vigil to honor lost strangers.

Bringer of Dawn

At points throughout my childhood, I saw my father be moved to tears. Sometimes this happened when he listened to a favorite piece of classical music or watched an elevating film. Sometimes it happened in prayer. Nevertheless, he always maintained his composure even as he opened his sensitive heart.

Clark and I were living in Newport, Rhode Island, when I heard my father truly let go and cry. He called to let me know that my Grandma Ellen, his beloved mother, had passed away. It wasn't an unexpected phone call as she had been receiving hospice care. Still, the news moved me. Listening to my father opened a vista for me to see fully into his sorrow. Every word he spoke cracked with wrenching sobs. For the first time in my life, I heard the brokenhearted little boy inside of my father weep.

I kept reliving the memory of the last time I saw my grandmother alive. Bent over with age and struggling with Alzheimer's, she washed apples in her kitchen sink. After a weeklong trip to Utah, Clark and I were visiting to say good-bye. I stood by her and watched her gracefully move her aged and bent fingers nimbly in the water. She had lovingly mothered seven children and remained a trusted confidant through their lives. A nurse by training, she embodied nurturing and gentle energy. My love for this kind woman filled me.

Grandma reached over to the drainboard. She took one of her white china cups and washed it. It didn't take long to realize that she thought the cup was an apple. She handed the china cup to me sweetly saying, "Take this with you, a healthy treat for the road." She always gave us fruit as a snack for the car ride home. Here she was, generous to the end, even though she couldn't tell the difference between the china cup and an apple.

Clark duly noted the tears welling in my eyes. He graciously took the cup from her wrinkled, veined hand. "Thank you, Grandma," he said gently. When she wasn't looking, he put it back on the drainboard.

Although it's human nature to sort through stories for meaning, I agree with Joseph Campbell when he asserts the supremacy of experience over meaning. He writes, "People say that what we are seeking is a meaning for life. I don't think that's what we're really seeking. I think that what we're seeking is an experience of being alive, so that our life experience on the purely physical plane will have resonance within our own innermost being and reality, so that we actually feel the rapture of being alive." The experience of my grandmother's heart-opening kindness and the experience of my father's heart-wrenching pain open me to life's rapture more than any theory about life and death ever could.

I miss my grandma. Even today, dreams and memories of her gentle presence inspire. Her handcrafted quilt rests on my bed, keeping me warm. She made it for me for my wedding. Whenever I see Taber look up and peacefully gaze at the ceiling, I smile. I imagine that he perceives the light of his great-grandmother's presence checking in on us. Whether or not angels exist, whether or not any element of Grandma Ellen lives on, I know one thing clearly -- without love we are irrevocably adrift.

In modern society, so many are disconnected from experiencing the power of life's most intense thresholds, the power of birth and death. So many women never witness childbirth until it is directly upon them, until they themselves are in labor. Death, like birth, is often cornered off into anonymous hospital rooms. Yet much wisdom exists in directly witnessing the transformative energies present in these thresholds. Much wisdom exists in holding space as the generations move through time. I faced many of my fears about death and birth by exploring these thresholds, by experiencing their power. I rely less on the construction of meaning as a result. As Campbell asserts, it is the experience of a life fully lived that matters. I've found that the experience of love transforms and heals. This truth shines unburdened by any metaphysical proclamation. It simply is.

*

Attached to my left hip and resting snuggly in his carrier, Taber spent the afternoon with me exploring downtown Philadelphia. At one point, we took refuge from the winter chill in a Catholic church. The golden tones of stained glass portraits added to the sweetness of carrying my little one throughout the day. We rested there. He nursed. I prayed for everyone to know such peace. On the way back to the train, we stopped to watch a crew of skateboarders perform cement-defying tricks. The free-spirited, longhaired boys made my tired little one laugh.

We were both weary after a full day. I looked forward to going home, putting Taber down for a nap, and meditating.

While waiting on the platform for our train, a young woman approached us. Dark roots and poorly applied red dye marked her greasy hair. Her long fingernails were painted with fading rainbows of mismatched colors. She smiled at us. I focused my gaze on her eyes. They were friendly and sad, and they sought connection. Taber snuggled in closer to me. I could have found a skillful way to ignore her, but I didn't. I looked at Taber. He trusted me with every cell of his tender goodness. My task was to navigate life's beautiful and treacherous waters with his wellbeing foremost in my consciousness. I placed a reassuring hand on Taber's back, and I chose to connect to the young woman.

Philosopher Nel Noddings offers wise counsel in such moments. When caring for another, she advises that we practice "motivational displacement." Central to her philosophy of care ethics, Noddings encourages us to set aside our own motivations and make time to truly listen. Echoing the wisdom of Saint Francis, she urges us to understand before seeking to be understood. Whether we care due to our nature or due to a cultivated sense of ethics, Noddings affirms a feminine approach to the task. She herself is the mother of five biological children, and she and her husband adopted five more. Imagine the orchestral-like organization required in this seamless combination of natural and ethical caregiving.

Doula work, hospital chaplaincy, and motherhood require motivational displacement. They also require the renewing light of mature care ethics. To give so fully, for so many hours, in such a deeply intimate and powerful way requires the giver to step back on occasion to fully recharge. Just as the moon waxes and wanes, so too must caregivers balance the offering of time and talent with the ability to receive inspiration and renewal. Of course, while massaging the feet of a birthing mother, holding the hands of a grieving wife, or reading a story to my son, I can choose to breathe mindfully. This immediately restores a momentary sense of balance and connection. It's vital to take the time to nurture a deep relationship with silence, mystery, and love.

I knew when I got home that I would have the time to rest, to care for self after our urban adventure. So I set aside my own agenda to daydream on the way home and focused on the life story unfolding in front of me.

At one point, the young woman described the drama leading up to her losing her job as a restaurant cook. Fired when a new owner took over, she lamented her unemployed status. "It's been really hard," she said. Currently, she could afford to eat only one meal a day. I offered her a banana from my backpack and continued to listen.

Taber nursed and this prompted her to ask questions about breastfeeding. "Does it hurt?" she asked. "How long should you breastfeed? Do you ever run out of milk?"

The train moved along. To answer her questions, I drew on my own experience and the wisdom of Dr. William Sears, who is known for his remarkable contributions to the field of attachment parenting. Sears encourages breastfeeding mothers to trust the inherent wisdom in their little ones. Nursing on demand honors the evolutionary dance that links mother to child. Both benefit tremendously through this attachment.

The young woman listened, smiled broadly, and said, "I think it's really special." Then she talked about her mother's lifelong neglect. "She said I wouldn't breastfeed." She shrugged.

I saw how the young woman's struggle extended all the way back to her earliest days of experiencing a trying attachment to her mother. How I wish a skilled lactation consultant had been available to guide her mother though those often challenging first few weeks of breastfeeding. I remember crying as I curled my toes in pain every time Taber latched as a newborn. "Don't give up Amy," Clark had said. "One day soon, nursing will be something you treasure." When my nipples started bleeding, we immediately set up a meeting with a lactation consultant. I remain forever grateful to this woman. Reaching out for informed breastfeeding support truly made all of the difference in the world for me. Within three days of our meeting, the pain was gone.

I understand that a small percentage of biological mothers truly cannot breastfeed. This is often due to contraindications with prescription medicine or a result of breast augmentation surgery. Also, a small percentage of babies struggle to learn how to latch properly, often due to being tongue-tied. Perhaps that was the case for this young woman. I tried not to judge. However, I do seek to change and challenge our culture's ambivalence toward breastfeeding. Plenty of well-documented medical studies note the plethora of health problems that trace back to the use of artificial milk, the chemical concoctions of infant formula. Human breast milk evolved perfectly. It is in our best interest to respect the milk that no formula can imitate. Newborn babies seek out breastfeeding and while the mother and child must learn how to nurse together, the instinct to latch is innate.

The young woman continued to share her story. Barely making it financially, she relied on unemployment checks while looking for prospective jobs on her cell phone. "They all want online applications," she lamented. "I can't afford an Internet connection in my apartment right now." I suggested seeking support and free online access at the local library. "I hadn't thought of that," she said. She finished the banana and got off at the next stop. From my seat, I watched her walk off the platform into the sprawl of neglected, blown-out buildings and faded graffiti. I wished her well.

Throughout the journey, Taber alternated between nursing, watching the world go by through the window, and connecting to fellow passengers. Few can resist a simple glance into his magical eyes and he took advantage of this fact in his efforts to initiate various rounds of peek-a-boo. He loved the attention. At one point, he reached out his tiny finger to touch the woman behind us. Her face was covered with burn scars. He smiled broadly at her. He could see through her disfigurement into her beauty. She smiled back. I once had my high school philosophy students go outside to examine their own shadows. We were reading Plato's "Allegory of the Cave" at the time. Yet, more powerful than any philosopher's edict, Taber's curious innocence reminds me to look to the light. I'm humbled to learn from this child. I'm both proud and protective.

For myself, I continued to think about the young woman and the stories she shared. I also know the pain of living with a mother wound. I know what it is like to struggle financially. Her many questions also inspired deep musings on my own understanding of breastfeeding at this point in my journey as a mother. I am so grateful I listened to her story.

For the first time in human history, the female breast is nearly completely separated from its primary mammalian function. Rather than supporting the healthy development of our limbic lives, breasts are pornographically used to market a multitude of products. Why is the breast's primary lactating function deemed strangely controversial today?

Despite the efforts of breastfeeding advocates, consider that mainstream news publications and talk shows feature mothers who nurse toddlers as cultural oddities. The American Academy of Family Physicians warns, "If the child is younger than two years of age, the child is at increased risk of illness if weaned." Yet only a small percentage of Western babies receive the life-sustaining gift of breast milk throughout their first year of life. In New Jersey alone, less than a third of babies are exclusively breastfed past their third month. This stands in stark contrast to tens of thousands of years of human evolution wherein children weaned at some point during their toddler years. Our own society's rupture from the wisdom of ancient ways is the true cultural oddity.

I applaud the efforts of public health advocates seeking to reconnect to the ancient wisdom of our female ancestors. Friends and family need to draw a fierce circle of protection and noninterference around the nursing mother-child dyad. "If nothing else, think optimal nutrition," my friend Jon said. A former Marine and a self-declared warrior for peace, he firmly supported his wife in nursing their sons during the toddler years.

If it were up to breastfeeding advocates, federal legislation mandating paid maternity leave would exist everywhere. For nothing pressures a new mother to give up nursing more than struggling to meet the financial needs of her family. While I was teaching in Colombia, my employer was obligated legally to give me three months of paid maternity leave. Yet if I had been working in the US at the time, it would have been up to my employer to determine the status of my maternity leave. The US stands alone as the only developed country without legally mandated paid maternity leave. This directly connects to our woeful breastfeeding rates.

Even though my mother breastfed all seven of her children as babies, I inherited the bias of my culture and formed harsh judgments about women who breastfed their toddlers. I had no idea what I was talking about. Falling in love with my son, trusting the process of nature, and participating in the mother-child nursing relationship offered a humbling awakening. Reading Gabrielle Palmer's *The Politics of Breastfeeding* fully opened my once egotistical and judgmental eyes. From my conversations with other breastfeeding mothers, I know I am not the only one who has experienced this needed paradigm shift.

In particular, Palmer's connections between poverty and breastfeeding moved me. Over the last century, the purposefully deceptive marketing ploys of infant formula makers have left tragedy in their destructive wake. For example, when promoting artificial milk in the developing world, companies dressed their representatives as medical professionals who claimed that their products were better than breast milk. Poverty-stricken and largely uneducated mothers were persuaded to spend a large percentage of their household's monthly income on the artificial milk powder that was considered best. To prolong its use, they often diluted the powder further reducing any nutritional value. In addition, these mothers lived in areas with poor sanitation and unsafe drinking water, from which the formula needed to be constituted. Palmer describes how hundreds of thousands of babies died. At times, I had to put the book down as angry tears washed through me.

Choosing to move beyond the painful disconnections of our culture, I do my best to support the breastfeeding mothers I meet. Our world must move beyond separating baby from mother, self from breath, and bodies from hearts. At night, Taber and I dive into dreamland together, as mothers and babies have throughout human history. His organic rhythms of rest and wakefulness mark my days. When he cries to communicate, he is heard. Clark and I respond with a surprisingly deep well of patience. Taber benefits from a hardy combination of the best of Clark and me, but his happiness directly correlates to the fact that his inborn biological need to nurse and be securely attached is lovingly fulfilled. People so often remark, "He's such a happy baby!" It's true. Taber exudes health and joy. It is not by accident.

While nursing, I read about human brain development. Again quoting from *A General Theory of Love*, "The infant's brain is designed for ongoing attunement with the people predisposed to find him the most engaging of all subjects, the most breathtaking potent axis around which their hearts revolve." My heart spins with this love. Breathing fully makes trusting ancient instincts possible. I take refuge in the intelligence of nature and a growing movement of modern mothers who co-sleep, breastfeed on demand, and practice the kindness of child-led weaning. I join them in trusting the body and trusting the baby. For the health of our future, we must honor the evolutionary links that bind mother to child and child to mother. We ignore this wisdom at our peril. In our humble home, Clark and I commit to honoring the natural rhythms of life. We strive to reconstitute what is currently torn asunder, whether found in society or in our own hearts.

To this end, I continue the painful process of honest self-reflection, if not for myself then certainly for Taber. My ability to mother him directly correlates to my own integration as a person. Memories of my mother and her current inability to be present in my life still sting. Places of anger, hurt, and frustration exist within me. I imagine they always will. What I can change is how I understand them. How do I welcome negative emotions with my breath when tightness grips my heart or belly? How do I love the parts of me once deemed unlovable?

Breastfeeding Taber offers pristine moments of clarity. I've cried many tears while watching my son nurse. Certainly I can have compassion for the woman who held me to her breast. How could she have known this sweetness and let fear close the door to her heart? I remind myself that she couldn't help it. I work to cultivate compassion given her profound inner struggle. I take refuge in the love I know that she has for me even if she can't express it. Despite my many flaws, I am so grateful for my mental wellbeing. I am able to let the pure love found in mothering Taber open and heal my once-troubled heart.

*

Today, the pea-sized toes of my son's plump foot rest on my belly. I nurse him. My skin is the boundary between his two known worlds. Not even a year ago, his foot existed on the other side of my skin. Clark and I often marveled at his fetal movements and energetic uterine kicks. Now, Taber playfully wiggles small toes in the air. It is a tender mercy to love this child. I regard his whole being as magically miraculous. When my own fetal-self nestled inside the life-giving body of my mother, part of him lived in me, too. My tiniest life-giving eggs, developing inside of my mother's body, carried half of his DNA. Generations nest inside each other. If that isn't a miracle, I don't know what is.

Tiny pink blood vessels constitute the artwork around my son's eyes. I marvel at his soft baby skin and admire his freshly cut toenails and fingernails. "He has little big hands," I tell Clark. "They will grow to be square-shaped and strong like yours." My husband's skillful hands can restore wooden boats, fly airplanes, fix a 1967 Land Rover, and even crochet. No doubt Clark's many pursuits and talents will inspire, but Taber will discover his own crafts. He will forge his own keys.

In Islamic theology, angels possess no free will. They simply love God. Humans can choose to love and for this reason our love is deemed higher than the love of angels. I treasure these early years of holding an angel to my breast. Taber loves; it is his nature. He hasn't learned to ignore, hold, or hide away his moving, pulsing, primal softness. No trauma or negative life event has hardened his heart with pain. He doesn't opt for love at this stage. He is love. He breathes light. Through a deep and abiding experience of our love, may he grow to choose love.

Sunlight washes over tree branches. Water rushes through neighboring streambeds over stones, under roads, finding the path of least resistance. Tonight's full moon promises to cast fertile hope on winter fields. All around this earth, new babies breathe and remind watchful eyes of ancient rhythms. Life energy flows in and out of the generations.

Clark dances with Taber while singing along to Randy Travis love songs. Rice pasta boils on the stove. I watch them together, my two loves. I breathe in these most precious, happy days. A softness of heart and belly evokes a kindness I didn't know possible. I pray to always remember this simple sweetness. May it be a beacon of strength for me when the inevitable troubles of life arise. When life's challenges fill me with sharpness, I vow to remember this moment—this soft, holy moment.

*

After leaving my own mother's womb, the first thing I did was breathe in. The last thing I'll do in this body is breathe out. Tragic cases exist of babies who die before any breath fills their tiny air sacs. They are stillborn, still-breath. As a chaplain, I've held the grieving mothers whose little ones knew death before birth, death before breath. For the living, breath is a loyal and sustaining friend. Breath takes us through spring's renewal, bright summer days, times of thanksgiving, and through the valleys of betrayal and loss. Breath knits the tapestry of time. It is the moving life force linking our entrance and exit. Breath is an impermanent and blessed wonder for which I am most extraordinarily grateful.

I watch Taber breathe. He inhales; I exhale. He exhales; I inhale. He naps. His long black lashes rest. The sweet, unmistakable fragrance of breast milk moves in and out of his tiny pink lips. I sit nearby, mesmerized by his beauty. An assortment of colorful toys cheerfully adorns the carpet. Meditation moves through me. Sleep moves through my little one. Silent peace fills the room. The rain blesses our home with a billion soft drops of liquid life. My breathing child inspires me to find refuge in a holy, timeless practice.

Two sides of my life merge in meditation, the changing Amy-self and the unchanging source of all. The wave and the ocean recognize their vital link. My belly rises and falls. I notice a quiet, precious stillness. I breathe in this tender mercy. Meditation reminds me to consciously connect to the sustaining life energy within, the nascent potentiality underlying all form. The same oceanic energy moving through my body, blood, and breath moves through my sleeping son. My task is to keep my awareness of the light within me as strong as possible so I may mirror to him his own.

In labor, I had pushed, pressed, and cried as his body slipped out of mine. Now the little body I once breathed for breathes into the air around me. The powerful breaths that moved me through labor rest in mutual rhythm with his own. After meditating, I lie down next to him and hold him close. Yes, the experience of love transforms.

Older women often stop to talk with me and admire Taber's eyes. They approach me in the store, on the train, or in the park. With a wistful longing to halt time's relentless passage, they lament, "It goes so fast, so fast." Sometimes these women will cry, grieving the ravages of impermanence with a baby-carrying stranger. Children remind us of the potential of a long journey, and elders remind us that all human journeys end. It makes sense to cry when honoring both ends of life's spectrum. Indeed, the pace of life's dance is enough to make the little boys inside of grown men weep.

I, too, am humbled by life's *allegro* tempo, but the truth is that time moves at this pace for all of us. My husband's life advances at the same speed as my son's. May I treasure time's journey across my husband's handsome face as much as I marvel at Taber's daily growth and development.

One evening as a chaplain, I was called to support the family of an eighty-year-old man. When I entered the room, I noted his lifeless body. He had just died. A breathing tube remained in his mouth. His elderly widow's thin frame was slumped in a wheelchair next to the bed. I held her hand. Married sixty-five years, she wanted to kiss him "one last time." I helped her stand. Trembling, she touched her beloved's face, so familiar to her worn hands. A mindful and compassionate nurse took out his breathing tube. I held the elderly woman's shaking body up as she bent forward. Their lips touched. Her tears fell on his skin.

Whenever I remember this story, I envision beloved lovers parted by death. I can only imagine what it was like for my grandfather to kiss my Grandma Ellen for the last time. In particular, I think of Clark. Daily, we say loving though casual good-byes to each other as we embark on our various tasks. What about the upcoming final good-bye? Who will bend to kiss the other's quiet lips? The memory of witnessing this powerful love story's conclusion remains one of the most moving experiences I had as a hospital chaplain.

Imagine a cosmic counting house full not of money but of breath. Each life is allotted a certain number of inhalations. Each day, all creatures make a withdrawal from the breath's bank, yet the total balance of remaining inhalations is hidden from view. One day, I will show up at this imagined center of cosmic commerce and time's teller will announce my account as empty. Death has withdrawn all funds. How will I respond to this news? Will I turn in anger? I pray to bow in gratitude for the grace of having known even one day. What if death comes to Taber before me? I quickly would transfer all of my future breaths to him if needed. When my time comes, I hope to say a conscious farewell to the beloved ones who have known and held me. I pray that spirit guides me as I say good-bye to my husband and my son, beings that I love beyond all measure.

I'll never get over the night sky's vast expanse that contains innumerable stars. It almost hurts to take in their wild and wondrous beauty. The sky's incredible capacity to silence my mind and transport me to a state of humility astounds me. I long to live fully awake in this dance of birth, breath, and death. I am not always brave enough to be so bold, but I am brave enough to try. May I see my son grow into an honorable and loving man. May I live a life I am proud to call my own.

Why should I strive to put these meditations into words? What seeks to merge with mystery? What exists behind and within this play of time and space? We dance between form and formlessness. Within our world's tumultuous light show of changing energy reside a grand mystery, a witnessing pulsation, and a quiet, still point of love. All of our beloved ones move through this light.

As a girl, I spent hours playing on the swing set in our backyard. I loved the freedom of soaring through the Utah mountain air. Today, I watch Taber with delight while we swing. He stands on my legs. I hold his back securely with one arm. We move together, gliding back and forth joyfully. I watch him arch his small body back as he completely trusts me. He looks at the twisting and turning branches above. He laughs out loud, dispelling all darkness. My boy, the bringer of dawn.

Q&A
with Amy Wright Glenn

First of all, what is a birth and/or postpartum doula?

A birth doula is a trained professional who offers skilled, informed, and loving support to a laboring woman and her partner. A birth doula is a guide through the birthing process as she draws upon proven comfort measures to support women in labor. Postpartum doulas work with new mothers and provide evidenced-based support with regard to breastfeeding and healthy mother-child attachment. In both capacities, doulas "mother the mother." I worked as a birth doula for six years before becoming a mother myself. I loved it.

What about doulas who work with the dying?

There is a growing interest in end-of-life or death doula work. Why? Death, like birth, is very medicalized in our culture. Given this, the holding of gentle, comforting, and supportive space for the dying is often sidelined. As founder of the Institute for the Study of Birth, Breath, and Death, I work diligently to inspire birth professionals to engage more formally with those of us who are trained in hospice or hospital chaplaincy. I also work to ensure that end-of-life care professionals benefit from conversations with birth and/or postpartum doulas. The Institute offers inspiring and nurturing professional development webinars, workshops, and trainings. Membership is open to all. We have much to learn from each other.

You share birth stories and reflect upon your work as a chaplain supporting the dying, but say more about the "breath" part of your book?

The first thing we do upon leaving our mother's body is breathe in, and the last thing we do upon exiting this world is breathe out. The breath is the link, the thread. Breath is a powerfully loyal friend throughout life's journey between birth and death.

I practice and teach yoga and meditation. Conscious breath awareness is central to these mindfulness practices. It's central to living a mindful life. The "breath" part of the book relates to teachings drawn from many wisdom traditions that help us live with love, appreciate beauty, and seek truth.

What inspired you to write Birth, Breath, and Death?

My husband, Clark, came up with the title of this book during my training as a hospital chaplain. He encouraged me to begin writing at that time. But I wasn't ready.

The birth of my son, Taber, compelled me to write this book. I didn't want to go back to full-time work upon holding Taber for the first time. I rebelled against any notion that would separate me from my newborn son. It took time to forge a new path. Yet I successfully drew upon my skills as a writer and yoga teacher to contribute financially to my family while fulfilling my heart's longing, and the longing of my young son, to stay at home and nurture him with the best of my energy and talents.

You studied comparative religion and taught this at the college and high school levels. How does this impact your writing?

My studies of comparative religion and philosophy profoundly impact everything I do. I love making links between the particular and the universal, between the day-to-day patterns of living and the deep reflections that thinkers across time and cultures bring to human life. My book is academically rigorous in the sense that I draw freely from my training as a scholar in the telling of birth, breath, and death tales.

Who will benefit from reading your book?

All of us are born. All of us die. We each encounter both the miraculous and the mundane. We are at the mercy of the energies of birth and death. Given this, we all benefit from reflecting upon life's big questions.

My hope is that mothers in particular will draw inspiration from this book. May my words encourage mothers to be empathetically responsive to their children, trust their feminine intuition, and draw upon best practices based on peer-reviewed studies in order to nurture the next generation with great love.

What do you feel is the purpose of life given that you've seen people be born and die?

Live. Love. Serve.

Live with an open heart. Love with fierce courage and commitment. Serve this world and all life.

That's what matters most.

Book Group Discussion Questions

Memoir and philosophy are woven together in *Birth, Breath, and Death*. Did this style of writing speak to you? What was it like to read stories and then examine their significance in light of ancient and modern philosophies?

Which chapter in Amy Wright Glenn's memoir spoke to you the most? Draw upon your own life experiences as you share your reflections.

Amy Wright Glenn describes birth and death as "sacred threshold points." Do you agree? What does she mean by "sacred"? What does this word mean to you?

As you read *Birth, Breath, and Death*, what emotions surfaced? Why?

What role does Amy Wright Glenn's mother play in this book? To what extent is it possible to heal from a "mother wound"?

The birth and death stories are clear enough in this account of doula work, motherhood, and chaplaincy. But what about the breath element in Amy Wright Glenn's writing? Where do you see breath at work in her stories?

Have you witnessed a birth? Have you held space for a death? Tell these stories.

For Further Reflection

Joan Borysenko, *Minding the Body, Mending the Mind*, Cambridge: DeCapo Press, 2007.

Joseph Campbell and Bill Moyers, *The Power of Myth*, Harpswell: Anchor, 1991.

Confucius, Raymond Dawson, translator, *The Analects (Oxford's Worlds Classics)*, Oxford: Oxford University Press, 2008.

"Doing Time. Doing Vipassana," Ayelet Menehmi and Eilona Ariel Directors. Karuna Film, 1998.

Richard Faulds, *Kripalu Yoga: A Guide to Practice On and Off the Mat*, New York City: Bantam, 2005.

Carol Gilligan, *In a Different Voice: Psychological Theory and Women's Development*, Harvard: Harvard University Press, 1993.

Daniel Goleman, *The Meditative Mind: The Varieties of Meditative Experience*, New York City: Tarcher, 1996.

Jonathan Haidt, *The Happiness Hypothesis: Finding Modern Truth in Ancient Wisdom*, New York: Basic Books, 2006.

Snatam Kaur Khalsa, *Grace*, by Spirit Voyage Music, Compact disc, 2004

David Kingsley, *Hindu Goddesses: Visions of the Divine Feminine in the Hindu Religious Tradition*, Berkeley: University of California Press, 1988.

Thomas Lewis, Fari Amini, and Richard Lannon, *A General Theory of Love*, New York City: Vintage, 2001.

Victor Malarek, *The Natashas: The Horrific Inside Story of Slavery, Rape, and Murder in the Global Sex Trade*, New York City: Arcade Publishing, 2011.

Rev. Peter Morales, editor, *The Unitarian Universalist Pocket Guide*, Boston: Skinner House Books, 2012.

Sachiko Murata and William Chittick, *The Vision of Islam*, St. Paul: Paragon House, 1998.

Nel Noddings, *Caring: A Feminine Approach to Ethics and Moral Education*, New York City: Teachers College Press, 2002.

Gabrielle Palmer, *The Politics of Breastfeeding: When Breasts are Bad for Business*, London: Pinter and Martin Ltd., 2009.

William Sears and Martha Sears, *Attachment Parenting: The Commonsense Guide to Understanding and Nurturing Your Baby*, New York City: Little, Brown and Company, 2001.

Penny Simkin, *The Birth Partner: A Complete Guide to Childbirth for Dads, Doulas, and All Other Labor Companions*, Boston: Harvard Common Press, 2007.

Peter Singer, *Practical Ethics*, Cambridge: Cambridge University Press, 2011.

Marilyn Sewell, editor, *Cries of the spirit: a celebration of women's spirituality*, Boston: Beacon Press 1991.

Thich Nhat Hanh, *The Miracle of Mindfulness: An Introduction to the Practice of Meditation*, Boston: Beacon Press, 1999.

Ken Wilber, *Grace and Grit: Spirituality and Healing in the Life and Death of Treya Killam Wilber*, Boston: Shambhala, 2011.

About the Author

Amy Wright Glenn earned her MA in Religion and Education from Teachers College, Columbia University. She taught in the Religion and Philosophy Department at The Lawrenceville School in New Jersey for over a decade. While at Lawrenceville, Amy was the recipient of the Dunbar Abston Jr. Chair for Teaching Excellence. Amy is a Kripalu Yoga teacher, Birthing Mama® Prenatal Yoga and Wellness Teacher Trainer, CD(DONA) birth doula, hospital chaplain, and founder of the Institute for the Study of Birth, Breath, and Death. Amy is a regular contributor to PhillyVoice and her work has appeared in numerous blogs and magazines. This is her first book.

To learn more, visit: www.birthbreathanddeath.com

Made in the USA
Lexington, KY
27 September 2015